M000286974

The pandemic has reiterated the significance of digitization in EVERYTHING we do, but more significantly in health care. It is indeed survival of the digital fittest. Ed and Paddy are expert practitioners in digital transformation who have synthesized several key trends and this book is a compelling narrative that defines the future of healthcare as we know it.

CP Gurnani
CEO, Tech Mahindra

The future of healthcare is now, as response to COVID-19 has shown us. Virtual, always available, and at home. Now it's up to us to make a new normal of care delivery liberating, highly efficient and effective. This book shows us a clear path forward in the midst of crisis.

Ashish Atreja, MD
Chief Innovation Officer, Mount Sinai Medicine

I recognized Ed's career potential when I hired him for his very first healthcare job – and Ed proved me right!

Mike Gogola
President, Florida Guardian ad Litem Foundation
Retired Global CIO

Many people talk about digital transformation, but few can actually make it a reality. It takes vision, courage and expertise to change the course of an organization. Ed and Paddy are practitioners of organizational digital transformation which gives them the refreshing perspective of veterans. The stories in Healthcare Digital Transformation are steeped in wins, losses and long hours of work with dedicated professionals focused on making healthcare better. This book is a roadmap for those who are ready to usher healthcare into the future.

Bill Russell
Managing Editor, This Week in Healthcare IT

Understanding digital is critical for any organization, especially as we move toward the post-pandemic era. This is a great roadmap for any Leader, regardless of industry. As an example, and what makes this book such a great tool/road-map; is each chapter includes a high-level 'consult' – practical ideas you can use to implement the concepts from the respective chapter.

Tom Hulsey
Author, The Winning Mindset that Saved my Life
Board Member, Mary Crowley Cancer Research

Can you embrace, then transcend what's tragic to build new opportunities for yourself, families, and networks leveraging technical shifts. This is how healthcare can become more efficient, precise, and physically distant – safe for clinicians and patients. Ed and Paddy have the expertise, know-how, and networks; Let them help light your path.

Sherrie Douville
CEO, Medigram, Inc.

A must read for all interested in digitalization and the future of healthcare IT. Written by a nationally recognized leader with professional integrity.

Arlene Anschel
Consultant, Witt Kieffer

Timely and inspiring! Our new digital world will require leadership that is innovative, courageous, passionate and effective. Ed and Paddy provide a roadmap that healthcare leaders must embrace.

Britt Berrett, PhD
Past Executive Vice President, Texas Health Resources
Professor, University Texas Dallas

With Ed and Paddy's depth and breadth of experience in the realm of healthcare innovation, this book should be the de facto handbook for any organization or leader that is on their journey for healthcare digital transformation.

Bradley Dick
Vice President, Ellkay

The ideas in this book were time tested, successful strategies that as the CEO of New York City Health & Hospitals and Ed, as chief digital officer, implemented during our process of digital transformation. The framework is foundational for success for any organization no matter where you are.

Ram Raju, MD
Former CEO, New York City Health & Hospitals
Senior Vice President, Northwell Health

The ability to combine experience and industry wisdom with a willingness to learn and change makes the difference between an organization that is on the leading edge and one that is not. Digital offers unique and valuable insights that will help technologists promote and support innovation and transform processes and cultures.

Pamela Arora
Children's Health, Senior Vice President and CIO
Board Member, HIMSS

This is a real-world practical playbook full of actionable insights around were we are now as an industry given the pandemic and what the next generation of Heath Care consumption and delivery will look like infused with digital technology and analytics. A must read for anyone that wants to lead transformation in the Healthcare industry.

Daniel Garrett
Retired PwC Partner
Board Member, Multiple Companies

An important book, at an important time. Highly recommend for healthcare professionals and investors.

Jared Sender
Investment Banker

Digital medicine is now medicine. Technology should increase the quality of the data available to physicians and enhance the consumer experience for patients. Edward and Paddy identify why healthcare is at an inflection point and how a digital transformation benefits all. This book outlines well why all providers should embrace the change and accelerate their digital transformation.

Daniel Barchi
Senior Vice President and CIO, New York Presbyterian

The pandemic has pushed the healthcare industry into the biggest disruption in decades forcing fundamental examination of how business and services are provided. Healthcare Digital Transformation is a forward-looking blueprint to navigate and "create" the future state. Ed Marx and Paddy Padmanabhan are uniquely positioned to write this timely and important book, as each have had extensive and varied experiences within large and complex healthcare organizations.

Matthew Hamlin
Vice President and General Manager, Quest Diagnostics

A man of tremendous faith, Ed Marx is an industry giant in the field of innovative healthcare. His latest literary effort is sure to be an excellent roadmap for leaders in all walks of life.

Thaddeus McCall
Pastor, Greater Love Mission Church

This is the timeliest book that not only provides the guidance to alter the slow spiral diminish of our industry, but rather prepares us with a roadmap and applies the intellectual capital to accelerate our transformation and embraces the digital world to exceed any other industry from the past.

Craig D. Richardville
Senior Vice President and Chief Information and Digital Officer, SCL Health

Once again, Ed paints a vision of what's possible coupled with a roadmap to guide the journey into the unknown and shifting sands of 'digital transformation' in healthcare. When we worked together in an evolving health care system, I found his ability to see into the future, and nudge those around him to step into his vision to be just what was needed to help us make tracks quickly. If you can't work directly with Ed, this is a close second best! Enjoy, Learn & Apply...and watch what happens...

Cheryl Lynn Mobley
President, reCalibrate LLC

The authors of Voices of Innovation are not only well-known innovators within the health technology industry, but they also have hands on practical experience in delivering solutions to some of the most prestigious healthcare organizations in the world. Whether you are an IT professional or not, this book will provide you with great insights into the complex world of healthcare.

Ivo Nelson
Entrepreneur, Author, Consultant

"Healthcare Digital Transformation" is a breath of fresh air for an industry that often keeps the windows closed. In their excellent book, Ed Marx and Paddy Padmanabhan make the case that for healthcare executives to grow, they must seek both knowledge and talent from outside the domain, looking to other industries for novel ways forward.

Anthony Guerra
Editor-in-Chief, HealthsystemCIO Media

Transformations are never easy, digital or physical. Everyone knows that the Healthcare industry needs a massive revamp. Ed Marx and Paddy Padmanabhan's book is a refreshing look at how one engages in an enterprise transformation that is based on a three-legged framework that sits on vast domain experience, process/method rigor and new age digital technology.

Dilip Keshu
CEO, BORN Group

The name Ed Marx is synonymous with healthcare information technology. Assembled through years of experience at some our nation's most preeminent health systems, together with a passion for the betterment of health and leadership, Ed and Paddy take us on a journey of digital transformation. An essential handbook for those seeking a primer in digital health.

Gene Mannheimer
Senior Research Analyst, Digital Health,
Healthcare IT & Services at Colliers International

Moving beyond having a deployed EHR to extending it, along with related technologies, to communicate and interoperate with all extended care givers, to enable analytics and predictive medicine and to truly Transform both your practice and your patient's lives is like moving from Ford's Model A, and rutted dirt roads to modern integrated, reliable transportation. Use this book as your roadmap!

Peter S. Tippett, MD, PhD
CEO careMESH

Never has a focus on innovation, transformation, and disruption been more relevant for healthcare than today. In the Keanu Reeves sci-fi "The Day The Earth Stood Still", his alien character postulates that "humans don't change until they are standing at the precipice". Right or wrong, Covid has brought us to that place, and has forced us to alter our course overnight, more than any pilot, experiment, or regulatory change has done in a decade or more. Leaders at CMS and insurance companies have rolled back archaic policies and rules that have stood in the way almost overnight, and I've heard from many physicians across the country that are realizing for the first time that quality care can be delivered digitally – in its variety of forms.

This book is a wonderful resource. Ed and Paddy have created an excellent construct for organizing and prioritizing, organizational planning, and moving forward. Based on their own experiences, the viewpoints of highly respected peers, and additional research and observation, it covers everything from basic blocking and tackling to implementing for the new normal. You are sure to derive some new thinking as well as validate and benchmark your goals and progress as a result of it!

Shelli Williamson
Senior Advisor, Scottsdale Institute

Healthcare Digital Transformation

How Consumerism, Technology and Pandemic are Accelerating the Future

Healthcare Digital Transformation

How Consumerism, Technology and Pandemic are Accelerating the Future

Edward W. Marx
and
Paddy Padmanabhan

CRC Press
Taylor & Francis Group
Boca Raton London New York

CRC Press is an imprint of the
Taylor & Francis Group, an **informa** business

A PRODUCTIVITY PRESS BOOK

First edition published 2021
by CRC Press
6000 Broken Sound Parkway NW, Suite 300, Boca Raton, FL 33487-2742

and by CRC Press
2 Park Square, Milton Park, Abingdon, Oxon, OX14 4RN

© 2021 Taylor & Francis Group, LLC

CRC Press is an imprint of Taylor & Francis Group, LLC

Reasonable efforts have been made to publish reliable data and information, but the author and publisher cannot assume responsibility for the validity of all materials or the consequences of their use. The authors and publishers have attempted to trace the copyright holders of all material reproduced in this publication and apologize to copyright holders if permission to publish in this form has not been obtained. If any copyright material has not been acknowledged please write and let us know so we may rectify in any future reprint.

Except as permitted under U.S. Copyright Law, no part of this book may be reprinted, reproduced, transmitted, or utilized in any form by any electronic, mechanical, or other means, now known or hereafter invented, including photocopying, microfilming, and recording, or in any information storage or retrieval system, without written permission from the publishers.

For permission to photocopy or use material electronically from this work, access www.copyright.com or contact the Copyright Clearance Center, Inc. (CCC), 222 Rosewood Drive, Danvers, MA 01923, 978-750-8400. For works that are not available on CCC please contact mpkbookspermissions@tandf.co.uk

Trademark notice: Product or corporate names may be trademarks or registered trademarks, and are used only for identification and explanation without intent to infringe.

ISBN: 978-0-367-47657-1 (hbk)
ISBN: 978-1-003-03569-5 (ebk)

Typeset in Garamond
by Deanta Global Publishing Services, Chennai, India

I dedicate this book to my five children who forced me to be digital. From the early days of MySpace to Instagram and beyond, you forced your Daddy to learn and grow. You taught me everything digital. Love you.

—Edward

This book is dedicated to those who work at the front lines of healthcare and save lives every day.

—Paddy

Contents

List of Figures and Tables

Figures

Tables

Foreword

Healthcare is experiencing a digital transformation that has
been decades in the making. Consumers are demanding convenience. COVID-19 responses exposed the need for further
automation, advanced analytics and rapid innovation. Big tech
players are moving in, intent on narrowing healthcare's technology gaps by leveraging artificial intelligence (AI), machine
learning, and advanced tools that other industries have long
embraced. Non-traditional players are also entering the market,
making bold moves that are disrupting incumbents.

To successfully navigate the digital transformation, healthcare requires forward-thinking strategic leaders who are willing to take charge, embrace technology-led innovation, and
boldly position their organizations for digital success. These
leaders must be passionate about their mission and committed to the development and execution of digital strategies that
position their enterprises for success and long-term relevance.

*Healthcare Digital Transformation: How Consumerism,
Technology and Pandemic are Accelerating the Future* is an
essential read for all healthcare leaders. While we have a
wealth of talented leaders, until now there's been a shortage
of roadmaps to guide organizations through the process. This
book, however, provides an agile blueprint for digital transformation success. Leveraging agile methodologies, organizations
can accelerate responsiveness to the market and public health,

making rapid, incremental progress aligned with enterprise strategy.

I can't think of two individuals more qualified to write this book than Edward W. Marx and Paddy Padmanabhan. Both have spent their careers promoting technology-led innovation in healthcare and have hands-on experience of developing and executing digital strategies. Individually, they are two of the industry's most highly regarded experts on this topic.

I was CEO at the Cleveland Clinic when I met Ed Marx. Ed was an experienced CIO who had held leadership positions at Texas Health Resources, University Hospitals, and the Advisory Board Company and had been recognized as the 2014 CHIME-HIMSS John E. Gall Jr. CIO of the Year.

In 2017, I hired Ed as CIO for the Cleveland Clinic. Though his title was CIO, Ed's true mission was to lead the health system's digital transformation. Over the next two years, Ed took charge, forged new trails, and worked to create a digital transformation framework. Under his leadership, the Cleveland Clinic developed its first digital strategy and began its execution.

Paddy Padmanabhan is one of healthcare's most widely published and quoted thought leaders on digital transformation, with long experience in the technology sector. In addition to his prolific writing, he leads a digital transformation and growth advisory firm and hosts *The Big Unlock*, a podcast series based on his book of the same name, featuring insightful conversations with some of the most prominent leaders in healthcare and technology today. His podcast is an essential resource for digital leaders in healthcare.

I first met Paddy when he asked me to be a guest on *The Big Unlock*. I was struck by Paddy's passion for the potential of new digital technologies, including the possibilities for reimagining the patient and caregiver experience, driving operational efficiencies, and enhancing the quality of life in our communities.

Together Ed and Paddy have created a handbook based on their in-depth, hands-on experience of leading health systems and technology firms. The book provides the specific "to-dos" to enable digital transformation in organizations, from initiating the journey to picking technology partners, establishing governance, preparing for future pandemics, and measuring results. Healthcare's digital transformation is in early stages. The insights they share in this book will benefit both healthcare and technology executives and enable enterprises to successfully navigate their digital transformation journeys.

Toby Cosgrove, MD
Former President and CEO of Cleveland Clinic

Acknowledgments

The idea for the book came together as the result of the work that Ed and I did together while he was CIO of Cleveland Clinic. I would like to start by acknowledging Ed for providing me that opportunity, and also to numerous other healthcare and technology executives with whom I have had the privilege of working over the past several years. Many of them have generously shared their insights with me through a series of formal and informal conversations, in particular as guests on my podcast, *The Big Unlock*. Their names are everywhere in the book. I want to especially acknowledge the support of Aaron Martin at Providence Health; Karen Murphy and John Kravitz at Geisinger Health; David Quirke at Inova Health; Daniel Barchi at New York Presbyterian; John Halamka at Mayo Clinic; Manu Tandon at Beth Israel Deaconess; Sylvia Romm at Atlantic Health System; Angela Yochem at Novant Health; Steve Miff of the Parkland Center for Clinical Innovation; and Dwight Raum at Johns Hopkins. The technology community has been enormously influential in accelerating the digital transformation of healthcare. I want to make a special mention of the deep insights I received from my conversations with Paul Black at Allscripts, Seth Hain and Sean Bina from Epic, along with a number of digital health entrepreneurs who are shaping the future of healthcare: Graham Gardner of Kyruus, Mike McSherry of Xealth, Mudit Garg of Qventus, Leah Sparks of Wildflower Health, and Drew

Schiller of Validic. Giovanni Monti of Walgreens gave me deep insights from the point of view of a non-traditional player in the healthcare market. John Glaser, who has been a mentor and an advisor, gave me a unique perspective from the point of view of a former healthcare CIO as well as a former senior executive with a major EHR company.

I want to thank the CHIME Foundation for supporting my firm's research which enabled us to interview dozens of healthcare executives for their experiences, all of which are in this book. Russ Branzel and his team deserve a special mention for all the work they do to advance healthcare IT.

My team from Damo Consulting supported me for the second time around with this book project, going above and beyond their normal duties. Special thanks to Arpita Bose Das, Kaushik Dutta, Bhawna Misra, and Sanjith Kumar for their editorial and design work. Katie McCandless, once again my manuscript editor, did a magnificent job of holding our feet to the fire on tightening up and streamlining the narrative.

Kristine Mednansky from Taylor & Francis gave us the start for this project and continued to support us through the inevitable ups and downs of writing and producing a book. We are grateful for her guidance, advice, and patience.

Last but not least, I owe thanks to my family who put up with my long absences during the writing of the book. They inspire me every day to be better.

Paddy Padmanabhan

This book is dedicated to all the teams I have served with throughout my healthcare journey. To the technicians and specialists who encouraged me as a 16-year-old janitor at the Peterson Air Force Base Medical Clinic. To my fellow Army 91B Combat Medic classmates who helped me learn our craft. To Poudre Valley Hospital for hiring me and giving me my first break. To Parkview Episcopal Medical Center for hiring me into my first IT-based role and helping me grow. To HCA for helping me develop enterprise vision. To University Hospitals of Cleveland for making a huge bet on me as a young CIO. Texas Health Resources for allowing me to take risks with innovation. To New York City Health & Hospitals via the Advisory Board for helping me fulfill my desire for public health. To Cleveland Clinic for the opportunity to be the first to lead digital and to allow me to serve in the operating rooms weekly as an anesthesia technician. Finally, to Tech Mahindra/ HCi for believing in me as the first global chief digital officer for health and life sciences. In each of these companies there was a team. All of the experiences and learnings that helped create this book came from them. Team of Teams.

A special shout out to our publisher and editors who helped shape the lumpy word clay into something readable to push our industry forward. My co-author Paddy for the book idea, his commitment to excellence, and a neverending supply of "red-eye" coffee with conversation.

Edward W. Marx

About the Authors

 **Edward W. Marx** is husband to Simran and father of Brandon, Talitha, Nicholas, Austin, and Shalani. He serves as the chief digital officer for TechMahindra/HCi Health & Life Sciences division. He has been blessed to serve as a CIO in many progressive organizations, namely, Cleveland Clinic, New York City Health & Hospitals, Texas Health Resources, and University Hospitals of Cleveland. Simultaneously, Edward began his distinguished military career starting as a combat medic and finishing as a combat engineer officer. Edward has written many books, including the bestselling *Voices of Innovation* (2019), *Scenes from an Early Morning Run* (2019), and *Extraordinary Tales of a Rather Ordinary Man* (2015). He is set to release a book on sexuality in marriage co-written with Simran (2020). In his spare time, Edward races for Team USA Duathlon and loves to hike and climb mountains with Simran. Edward received his bachelor's in psychology and master's in design, merchandising, and consumer sciences, all from Colorado State University.

Paddy Padmanabhan is an award-winning business leader and a trusted C-suite advisor with a proven history of success in guiding key strategies across the healthcare and technology sectors. He is the CEO of Damo Consulting, a digital transformation and growth advisory firm focused on the healthcare sector. Both commercially astute and entrepreneurially adept, Paddy has garnered a reputation for driving growth and efficiencies in both large corporates and start-ups within the healthcare technology industry. A visionary leader and practitioner, he has worked at globally recognized firms such as Accenture, GE, and Wipro where he built large global technology businesses and spearheaded strategic growth initiatives. He has also been in Silicon Valley start-ups that went through successful exits. A respected and credible voice in healthcare technology, Paddy is widely considered a thought leader and expert practitioner in digital transformation and growth strategy. He is the author of *The Big Unlock* – Harnessing Data and Growing Digital Health Businesses in a Value-Based Care Era and hosts a widely acclaimed podcast featuring C-suite executives from healthcare and technology. He is widely published and quoted in industry publications and has a long-running by-lined column in CIO magazine on digital health technology trends. He lives in Chicago.

Introduction

Over the last three years, the two of us have worked together to develop an enterprise digital strategy and roadmap for one of the top health systems in the country. We have separately worked with leading regional and national health systems on digital transformation initiatives. We have helped health systems with strategic technology choices in building their digital experience platforms for the future, and have spoken extensively on digital transformation at leading industry conferences. We have covered the topic in-depth in Paddy's book *The Big Unlock: Harnessing Data and Growing Digital Health Businesses in a Value-Based Care Era* and Ed's bestselling book *Voices of Innovation*, which included contributions from 57 healthcare industry leaders and technology vendors. Our hands-on work in developing and executing enterprise digital strategies, as well as our conversations with over 150 healthcare technology executives (chief executive officers, chief information officers, chief digital officers, and chief innovation officers), has greatly informed our view of what a digital transformation playbook could look like for healthcare enterprises.

We recall when dotcom became the rage, followed by e-commerce and then mobile. Mobile was followed by cloud computing and artificial intelligence, ultimately leading to where we are today: digital. While these stages are easy to understand, a different set of bold business concepts emerged that caused a fair amount of confusion: *innovation, transformation*, and *disruption*. When you combine the technologies with these concepts, the potential sounds promising. Ultimately these combinations of technology and business concepts led us to digital transformation. Business and technology leaders could understand mobile or cloud, given they were tangible assets. Harder to articulate and execute were emerging concepts such as innovation, transformation, and disruption.

There are scores of books about innovation. Yet few healthcare companies differentiate themselves accordingly. We are afraid of the same thing happening with transformation, specifically digital transformation. We have already seen the emergence of articles, essays, and books on digital transformation. Few help the reader develop plans to execute, however. The words written – much like with innovation books previously – are theories, not actions.

How do you enable and lead a digital transformation? How do you develop plans for it? How do you govern? Execute? Focus? How do you know when you've hit the target, closed the gap, and pleased the customer? What is digital nirvana?

When the COVID-19 pandemic hit us in early 2020, all these questions became urgent corporate priorities. Healthcare executives were compelled to change overnight in to respond to the twin challenges of treating hundreds of thousands of patients infected with the Coronavirus while keeping healthcare workers at the frontlines safe from falling victim to the infection themselves.

How can we prepare ourselves and our organizations for a digital transformation?

It is not the technology that holds healthcare back, but the culture. Given the implications of unintended consequences on patient care, healthcare is slow to change. Steeped in tradition, healthcare largely promotes from within, unintentionally limiting fresh ideas that stifle change. Afraid of errors, we insist on extended analysis before making decisions. Digital transformation leaders had to break through their traditional mindset and take risks and lead boldly. They develop alliances and partnerships, pursue curiosity, and push boundaries. It is no secret that healthcare lags behind other industries in embracing advanced technologies. If we don't grab hold of the digital transformation potential, the gap will widen and never close. Non-traditional and big tech entrants will fight for market share. Innovative start-ups, unencumbered by technical debt and bureaucracy, will leapfrog traditional players. Yet healthcare enterprises are in the best position to lead and seize the advantage, given their long-standing trusted brand names and historic patient loyalty. While there are many reasons for being a laggard outside of the healthcare leaders' control, this is never an excuse not to lead forward. While CIOs are in a strong position to lead digital transformations, it is no longer an assured path. Witness the emergence of the chief digital officer (CDO) and the corresponding reduction of the CIO's role and responsibilities.

We have listed below several tangible steps that leaders can take to better position themselves in the digital transformation era. While this list is incomplete, it is a good starter set of attributes and actions we have witnessed with effective leaders. Following these steps will help you remain relevant and lead the digital transformation.

You can't lead what you don't live: survival of the digital fittest.

Reverse Mentor: We all know the value of mentoring. Ideally, we give and receive. One of our mentors is a recent Denver University MBA grad. Jordan is a digital native and leads digital transformation for his family's communications company. Jordan teaches us advanced social engagement skills, along with the millennial experience and expectations.

Work: To lead digital transformation in a healthcare enterprise, we must know the clinician and patient experience. As an anesthesia technician, Ed prepares for surgical cases long before sunrise. He has developed numerous disruptive ideas that have made their way into the enterprise strategy by serving on clinical teams.

Volunteer: Ed is a recent cancer survivor. He is overly familiar with the patient experience. Even so, he continues to volunteer weekly. He needs the experience to be fresh. It cleanses the soul and recalibrates his true north. His patients teach him, remind him, and motivate him.

Experience: Paddy is a technology practitioner who has been in healthcare for the past 20 years in leadership roles with global tech firms and start-ups. He has worked as a trusted advisor to healthcare CIOs, and more recently, chief digital officers and chief innovation officers. He has seen up close the emerging digital transformation of healthcare from the perspective of healthcare organizations and technology solution providers who seek to serve them. Paddy sees the chasm between what solution providers think their clients want and *what they actually want*. He has seen the general confusion around what "digital" means. He has seen health system leaders actively seek the benefits of digital innovation while being fearful of the excessive hype by technology vendors overpromising and coming up short.

Peers: Learn from others' experiences. Seek time with them. Make an effort to discover best practices. Each year we identify digitally advanced organizations inside and outside of healthcare. We take our teams and spend the day with them, learning everything we can. We conduct exchange programs. Paddy's podcast is another platform to learn from leading practitioners of digital transformation. As a result, our digital capabilities grew, and matured exponentially.

Study: Use free time soaking up knowledge. Mobile publications are perfect on the plane. News aggregators save time and enable topic specificity. Both of us have researched our topic extensively. As a long-time CIO, Ed developed a deep understanding of how to implement technology-led transformations in healthcare and is sought out as a keynote speaker and an influential voice on information technology in healthcare. In addition to his consulting and advisory work, Paddy has written over a hundred opinion pieces on the topic of digital health technology trends and has a long-standing column in *CIO* magazine. Between us, we have collaborated on and published two previous books on this topic.

Observe. Always watch. Watch other leaders, especially from different industries, and ideally from other sectors recognized for digital transformation. Spend half your time outside of your industry. Yes, half. Leadership is humility. Just ask.

Advisory/Boards: Accept invites. Time is precious, but time invested in learning multiplies. Learn from digitally enabled vendors/partners. Develop relationships with leaders. Ask questions. Where is technology headed? How is their company leveraging digital? What are they doing personally to be digital? Then listen, deeply. Over the years, we've sat at the feet of CEOs from IBM, Cisco, HP, Google, Microsoft, GE, Tech Mahindra, and many smaller companies, unashamedly soaking up all the wisdom we could gather.

Be agile: Throughout our experience of working together and researching for the book, we found that those who make the most progress the most quickly are agile in their approach to innovation and transformation. Agile is all too often associated with software development; however, what we have found is that every aspect of digital transformation – people, process, and technology – needs to be led with an agile mindset.

To lead a digital transformation, you must exude digital. How can you pour out digital if you are an empty vessel? Reverse mentor, study, research. Work with your customers. Volunteer helping your customers. Observe others. Learn. Invest to understand the experience. You know technology. Now begin with yourself. Be digital. You will start to intersect technology purposefully. Transformation begins. Disruption is enabled. Changed self. Changed organization. Changed outcomes. Changed industry. Digital is personified in you.

What can we learn from other industries?

Healthcare is incestuous. When hiring talent, organizations require that candidates have 10 years of this kind of healthcare experience or 20 years of this other kind. Balderdash! If we are already behind, why do we keep hiring from the same pool? There are two practical steps here to take.

Hire from outside of healthcare. Make it a goal that half your team is new to healthcare. In other words, their role with you is their first in healthcare. We have enjoyed great success hiring from different industries such as finance, military, manufacturing, and entertainment. When you hire the right person, they can easily make the transition and understand the nuances of healthcare. That does not take long. When they combine their previous experience with technology and healthcare, transformation occurs. Stop hiring each other! Interestingly, many of the CDO hires in 2018 and 2019 came from consumer goods and services companies.

Stop going to healthcare conferences. We have many associates who strictly attend healthcare conferences. While it's important to remain connected to healthcare and industry peers, 50 percent of your time should be spent with peers outside of healthcare. We both have studied extensively what the more advanced sectors such as banking, hospitality, and manufacturing are doing with digital transformation. We recommend attending the annual Consumer Electronics Show and expanding your vision. Engage in conferences that push your buttons and boundaries and force you out of your comfort zone. Build your creative capabilities.

Accept non-healthcare advisory opportunities. Nearly every vendor company has an advisory committee.

Participate and push into all that are not industry-specific. We have been part of committees from Cisco, HP, and Microsoft, as well as digital health start-ups. Sitting to our left and right were non-industry peers from around the world. Learn what your peers in other industries are doing to transform digitally. Then adopt and adapt. Many of the most innovative digital health start-ups we spoke with for this book approached the traditional and gnarly problems of healthcare by observing how other sectors such as manufacturing, airlines, and even professional sports have brought about a step change in results.

This book is intended to be a playbook and reference guide for healthcare executives and the technology provider ecosystem. You will deepen your understanding of the current state of digital transformation and learn how to develop a digital transformation roadmap for the enterprise. Chief information officers, chief digital officers, chief innovation officers, and other C-level executives with responsibility for driving the digital transformation of the enterprise will find valuable insights from the work of their peers in the healthcare and technology worlds.

Digital transformation means different things to different people. However, there is one thing about it that everyone agrees on: it is a multi-year, evergreen, collaborative effort among stakeholders within the enterprise and strategic partners from the outside.

The framework and best practices referenced in this book are largely drawn from our work in health systems. However, health insurance and life sciences executives will find the contents equally relevant. Technology solution providers who play a critical role in enabling digital transformation for their client organizations will find that the book enriches their understanding of how healthcare executives are approaching digital transformation. We also cover what other technology providers are saying about the current state of digital and the opportunities ahead.

We recommend that you read the chapters in the sequence in which they are presented. We have summarized key take-aways and action items at the end of each chapter if you want to skip ahead for the important points. We have infused each chapter with insightful vignettes from practicing CIOs, chief digital officers, and other C-level executives who are carry-ing the digital transformation mandate for their organizations. We have referred extensively to our research as well as that of highly regarded institutions and analyst firms that track and monitor the healthcare sector. We have included contradic-tory viewpoints wherever we have felt they are relevant for the reader.

Throughout the book, we have used the terms EMR and EHR interchangeably, primarily based on how healthcare exec-utives have used the words during our interviews. Technically, EHRs refer to health records across multiple healthcare set-tings, whereas EMRs refer to records from a single setting. We don't believe the interchangeable use of these terms makes a material difference for this book.

The terms "digital" and "digital transformation" are closely related to one another, as are the terms "digital health" and "digital medicine." We have chosen to use the terms somewhat flexibly in the commentaries throughout the book without los-ing the essence of their meaning.

While the book primarily addresses health systems, we have frequently referred to them as healthcare organizations, which include health plans and other parts of the healthcare economy.

At the time of writing, many health systems are in the early stages of their digital transformation journeys. While the COVID-19 pandemic has accelerated awareness and response, there will be a season for reevaluation and reflection leading to adjustment. There is much confusion about the term "digi-tal" and what it means for health systems, their CEOs, CIOs, and the organization as a whole. We hope this book provides some answers and a roadmap for the way ahead.

The book draws from proprietary and public research. We conducted over 150 interviews with executives in leading health systems and technology providers over the past two years, and these have provided us with the core insights that you will learn in this book. The important role of emerging technologies, pandemic, EHR systems, digital health innovations, and big tech firms in the ongoing digital transformation of healthcare is explored through case studies of successful digital initiatives.

We reached out to numerous colleagues in the healthcare and technology sectors for their feedback and input on this book. They have been very supportive of this project and extremely generous with their time and input. We thank them for their support, and we have included their experiences and insights throughout the book.

Writing this book has been an illuminating and transformative experience for us. We hope it will help you and your organization accelerate your transformation journey, especially in the new and present reality of pandemic.

Edward W. Marx and Paddy Padmanabhan

Chapter 1

How the Covid-19 Pandemic Reshaped Healthcare with Technology

John Kravitz, CIO of Geisinger Health, a leading health system with 11 campuses and 13 hospitals in Pennsylvania, speaks about how the organization's leaders were "blown away" by how technology stepped up to help address the COVID-19 crisis. Geisinger's IT organization responded to a 500% increase in telehealth visits and enabled a doubling of remote workers to 13,000 employees in the initial weeks of the pandemic.

The Cleveland Clinic, long viewed as the leader in telemedicine, went from 2% to 80% of all outpatient visits being done virtually. Stories like Geisinger and the Cleveland Clinic played out across the country in the spring of 2020 as digital technologies – telemedicine in particular – definitively reshaped care delivery practically overnight. The Coronavirus crisis may have been a tipping point, if we look across time horizons for the future of healthcare, for how we live and work, and even the future of the planet.

The sudden upscaling of virtual care capacity: Front line healthcare workers were swamped in the initial days of the coronavirus outbreak by the number of calls from patients who want to speak with their doctors about possible symptoms for COVID-19. Many health systems quickly turned to self-triaging tools to help consumers check for symptoms before asking to be put through to a doctor. Providence Health in Washington State, which was Ground Zero for the pandemic in the United States, reconfigured their chatbot Grace* with FAQ's related to COVID-19 symptoms. Sara Vaezy, Chief Digital Strategy Officer at Providence Digital Innovations Group, states that they saw 70,000 patient logins and over one million messages come in through the chatbot in the first week of the outbreak. To put the numbers in perspective, that was 10 to 15 times more than pre-pandemic levels.

However, the challenge did not end there. Patients who got triaged for Covid-19 screening as possibly infected had to wait in a virtual queue because of the sudden spike in the number of virtual visits. The lack of available trained clinicians to take on virtual consults exacerbated the problem. To address the surge, Providence Health redeployed their same-day Express Care clinicians to attend to the newly triaged patients coming in through the chatbots. Elsewhere in the country, health systems went through some variation of this scenario. As health systems streamlined their processes and brought more clinicians on board, the learning curve began to flatten out as did new infections of the pandemic.

Not all online triaging tools are seeing the same levels of success. Silicon Valley tech firms, always quick to respond with technology to marketplace needs, have seen a lukewarm response to new tools by startups and big tech firms. Google parent Verily's symptom triaging tool for Covid-19 came under

---

* "Digital front doors – the new battleground for the healthcare ...." Accessed May 11, 2020. https://www.cio.com/article/3411919/digital-front-doors-the-new-battle ground-for-the-healthcare-consumers-attention.html.

criticism* from privacy advocates, highlighting the lack of trust that epitomizes the challenges for digital health companies in general. The same holds true by Google and Apple's attempt at convincing the public to leverage their contact tracing tool.

The mainstreaming of telehealth: Out of every crisis, a new opportunity arises. For telehealth, the COVID-19 pandemic was an opportunity whose time had finally come. The volumes of telehealth consults went up several multiples in the immediate wake of the pandemic for every hospital in the country as every facility shut down for all routine care. Elective surgeries were cancelled or postponed indefinitely. In anticipation, Geisinger Health trained over 1000 providers in a very short time on conducting telehealth visits with patients. Telemedicine platforms also enabled patient families to speak with their loved ones in acute care. While most health systems successfully scaled up their telehealth operations, some saw a rise in wait times that negated the premise of "on-demand" care through virtual health tools. In one case, the Cleveland Clinic,† the technology struggled to keep up with a 10x increase in volumes.

The use of telehealth has been growing in the past few years, though more slowly than expected. One major cause has been the lack of a reimbursement model for telemedicine that puts it on par with in-person visits. Recognizing the need to promote telehealth as a public health and safety issue, the Government has brought reimbursements for telehealth on par with other visits. A second major barrier largely eliminated was the need for clinicians to be licensed in every state for which they saw patients. Most states have relaxed their border -specific licensure laws to enable widespread

---

* "Alphabet's COVID-19 project underscores privacy concerns ...." Accessed May 11, 2020. https://www.modernhealthcare.com/operations/alphabets-covid-19-project-underscores-privacy-concerns-big-tech.

† "Telemedicine companies struggling to meet coronavirus ...." Accessed May 11, 2020. https://www.cnbc.com/2020/03/16/telemedicine-companies-struggling-to-meet-coronavirus-demand.html.

care. We may be seeing a tipping point that takes telehealth mainstream in one stroke, transforming the way we experience healthcare in the future. Most importantly, the public at large will get used to telehealth visits as an acceptable way of obtaining healthcare for low-acuity needs.

A related area of growth has been remote patient monitoring (RPM) and home monitoring. While RPM has grown steadily in the past couple of years, the shelter-at-home restrictions across the country during the pandemic have highlighted the need to monitor patients with chronic conditions in their homes. Hospitals put patients under investigation (PUI) who are suspected of having been infected with Covid-19 under close monitoring. The government and other important payors began more robust reimbursement for RPM as well.

Digital transformation of healthcare is on an accelerated path: While the pandemic caused some degree of reprioritization of ongoing enterprise IT projects in some health systems, others, such as UPMC and Geisinger Health in Pennsylvania, were accelerating* their digital transformation roadmaps, encouraged by the success of telehealth in responding to the crisis and also sensing a fundamental shift in healthcare delivery. Health systems caught off-guard by the sudden impact of an unprecedented national lockdown, realized that the future of their enterprises was at stake if they did not quickly pivot from a predominantly offline to an online mode of engaging with their patients and consumers. Realizing that there were going to be permanent shifts on healthcare delivery as a result of the pandemic, health systems also looked closely at aspects of routine and low-acuity care that could potentially be delivered through a combination of synchronous and asynchronous communication technologies.

---

* "Geisinger, UPMC among health systems fast-tracking tech ...." Accessed May 11, 2020. https://www.fiercehealthcare.com/tech/health-system-cios-covid-19-resp onse-we-ve-never-experienced-anything-like.

How we live and work have changed forever: At the time of writing, there were international efforts underway to develop a vaccine for the coronavirus. In the meantime, we have crossed a tipping point that is playing out through how companies are reorganizing their workforce around virtual workplace models, using video conferencing and other virtual collaboration tools to keep them safe from infections. As employees and employers get serious about maintaining productivity and effectiveness in the current crisis, companies and public health agencies will also apply the learnings from the present crisis to find ways to repurpose existing assets in preparation for the next crisis. During the pandemic, hotels turned into makeshift hospitals; sport and concert arenas turned into logistics hubs. In future, all new buildings may well require a degree of "repurposability" for pandemic preparedness. The benefits to society from such a shift are more profound. Reduced travel and commutes will reduce carbon emissions, paving the way for a reversal of climate change.

The future is here but is unevenly distributed, as someone said. The upsides from the crisis will seem minimal to the airline industry as it deals with grounded airplanes and a slow recovery in passenger travel. The rise of telehealth will mean little to local economies and small businesses; the millions who lost their livelihoods due to the crisis: the Ubers and Lyfts, the coffee shops and restaurants, and thousands and thousands of other service businesses. Our fellow humans in the margins of society may have to bear a disproportionate burden from the devastating health and economic impacts of the crisis. The FCC launched a $200 million* telehealth investment fund specifically targeting programs that would increase telehealth access to under-served and socially vulnerable sections of the population. At the time of writing, fears of an

---

* "FCC Fights COVID-19 with $200M; Adopts Long-Term ...." Accessed May 11, 2020. https://www.fcc.gov/document/fcc-fights-covid-19-200m-adopts-long-term-connected-care-study.

extended recession loomed large on the public consciousness. The worst of the pandemic may be behind us and the worst of the economic impact may be yet to come. Human resilience is being put to test – once again.

Until the COVID-19 pandemic, relative to other sectors, healthcare had been slow to adopt digital technology. A decade spent digitizing patient medical records with electronic health record (EHR) system implementations has left many health systems unable or unwilling to invest in a new round of technology transformation initiatives. However, consumer expectations, pandemic, and changing marketplace dynamics leave health systems with limited options. New and non-traditional competitors are emerging, many with comparatively unlimited resources and advanced technology capabilities, determined to reshape the markets. Many health systems have defaulted to their EHR systems to drive digital initiatives. Others are actively driving digital health innovation in focused areas such as telehealth and patient access. A handful of leading health systems are reimagining their business models and driving digital transformation across all enterprise functions. Consumerism, pandemic, and technology evolution is driving significant change.

Assessing the Current State of Digital Maturity in Healthcare

Digital is like democracy. Ask any two individuals for a definition of democracy, and you will get responses that broadly talk about representational government, one-person-one-vote, and periodic elections. If the two individuals happen to be from different countries, you will get definitions that reflect the particular variation of democracy for each individual. For instance, in India, where Paddy was born and raised, general elections happen every 5 years. In India, they do not elect their Prime Minister directly but indirectly through the party of their choice, unlike in the United States where citizens vote directly for a Presidential candidate.

So, it is with digital. The reality is that there is no universally accepted definition of digital just as there is no universally accepted digital maturity model.

What does the ideal healthcare experience of the future look like?

Over the past few years, we have seen several significant changes in the market for technology-led innovations in healthcare. "Digital health innovation" and "digital transformation" are terms commonly used to describe the changes healthcare organizations need to make for the future. Leaders and teams charged with driving digital transformation in healthcare enterprises face the same basic questions: What is digital? What does digital mean to the CEO and the board of directors? What does digital mean to the broader organization? What does it mean to peer group health systems across the country? Across the globe?

To put digital transformation in context, we need to understand the structure of the healthcare industry and how health systems make money. For most health systems, healthcare is a cross-subsidized business. Health systems make money on the commercial side of the business, which serves populations covered by employer-provided insurance or under parts of government-run programs. Most health systems lose money on Medicaid and Medicare, not to mention uninsured populations with no ability to pay. To sustain the organizational mission of supporting the poor and vulnerable, health systems must do an exceptionally good job of engaging the commercial population, keeping them healthy with preventative care. This part of the healthcare business is most at risk of being disrupted by emerging non-traditional players focused on more profitable commercial populations. Their primary differentiator is disruptive digital health tools. They concentrate on the user experience, ensuring simplicity and convenience and lowering costs while increasing engagement.

The biggest opportunity from healthcare's digital transformation is the elimination of friction in the healthcare value chain. Recognizing this opportunity, digital health start-ups have proliferated in the last few years. There is no question that we are seeing a shift in how healthcare is being delivered through new digital health solutions. Telehealth is growing, as is remote monitoring. According to the American Hospital Association (AHA), as of early 2019, 76 percent of hospitals in the United States connected with patients at remote locations through video and related technologies.* Data from increasingly diverse sources such as sensors and devices are being aggregated and combined with those from traditional sources such as electronic health records. Advanced analytical tools are available to process the data with low-cost infrastructure on the cloud to develop and deliver insights at the point of care. "We are accumulating a tremendous amount of data in healthcare. It gives us the ability to bring science to healthcare," says Dr. Toby Cosgrove, who served as CEO and president of the Cleveland Clinic (2004–2017), the number-two-ranked hospital in America, and who led the $8 billion organization to new heights of achievement and efficiency.

Digital transformation allows for a blend of art and science to enable a better experience for both patients and providers. Despite the promise, digital transformation faces several headwinds. The shift from fee-for-service to value-based care has not been as rapid as expected. According to a report by the nonprofit organization Catalyst for Payment Reform, an overwhelming majority of value-oriented payment – 90 percent as of 2017 – is built on a fee-for-service foundation, and just 6 percent of the total dollars as of 2017 flowed through payment methods that pose a downside financial risk to providers. This has remained relatively consistent since 2012, when it was

---

* "Fact Sheet: Telehealth." American Hospital Association. February, 2019. Accessed January 7, 2020. www.aha.org/system/files/2019-02/fact-sheet-telehealth-2-4-19.pdf.

5.7 percent.* Falling reimbursements in an era of accountable care have led to diminishing margins for health systems. This leaves little cash for discretionary spending on technology moving forward.

The entire healthcare sector is in the midst of consolidation, and the threat of disruptive non-traditional players looms large. Technology execution risk remains high due to the early stage of maturity for digital health solutions. Long years of underinvestment in technology, as well as vulnerability to security threats, mean that scarce resources are being consumed in order to address technical debt. As incumbents in every sector face disruption by a tidal wave of digitally enabled competitors, the writing on the wall is clear for healthcare enterprises: It is about survival. Consider the following trends.

A shift is occurring toward the virtualization of healthcare. With a hospital bed utilization rate of 65.9 percent[†] considered to be low, it is estimated that the majority of communities remain over-bedded today. It is expected that the number of hospital beds will continue to decline steadily in the coming years. As a result, more patients who are chronically ill will be treated at outpatient facilities and sent home the same day. In the past, they would have been revenue-generating in-patient admissions. Many surgeries that required hospitalization are now performed at ambulatory facilities.

Especially with the pandemic experience in 2020, the ability to find ways to treat people remotely through tele-health will continue to gain importance. Telehealth, which has largely been built around low acuity care, will evolve and

---

* "Payment Reform Has Grown Significantly, Though Not Across Methods Likely to Transform Health Care; Key Indicators Raise Questions About Impact to Date." Catalyst for Payment Reform. December 4, 2019. Accessed December 13, 2019. www.catalyze.org/about-us/cpr-in-the-news/new-national-scorecards/.

† Elflein, John. "Hospital Occupancy Rate in the U.S. from 1975 to 2017." Statista. December 9, 2019. Accessed December 13, 2019. www.statista.com/statistics/18 5904/hospital-occupancy-rate-in-the-us-since-2001/.

pivot toward higher acuity care, specifically toward patients with chronic care needs and limited mobility. Many routine healthcare services are now accessible via "digital front doors," for example, smartphone applications with intuitive user interfaces.

Vast amounts of venture capital are pouring into digital health. The opportunity to transform the inefficient and expensive healthcare system in the United States (18 percent of GDP and twice as expensive as the next Organization for Economic Co-operation and Development member-country in per capita healthcare costs) has attracted technology entrepreneurs in large numbers to healthcare. Venture capital firms poured $7.4 billion into digital health start-ups in 2019. A string of initial public offerings (IPOs) from maturing start-ups as well as M&A activity in the digital health space indicate a coming of age for many firms.

Funding levels serve as a validation of the potential of digital health innovation and the opportunities in the digital transformation of healthcare. Several high-profile IPOs, such as Livongo and Health Catalyst in 2019, point to a maturing start-up ecosystem. At the same time, many start-ups are struggling, and exits are not keeping pace with expectations. A few such as Theranos, Outcome Health, and uBiome have gotten into trouble* while trying to find shortcuts to growth and profitability. While funding levels declined in the wake of COVID-19, the promise of accelerated digital transformation could reveal several winners as well as new startups with solutions to the emerging challenges of virtual care.

New data sources and data interoperability standards are driving digital health innovation and healthcare outcomes. "We're all on a journey to turn data into information, knowledge, and wisdom," says John Halamka, President

---

* Schencker, Lisa and Ally Marotti. "Outcome Health Investors Receive DOJ Subpoenas as Chicago-Area Hospitals Back Away." *Chicago Tribune*. November 10, 2017. Accessed December 13, 2019. www.chicagotribune.com/business/ct-biz-outcome-losing-doctors-20171110-story.html.

of the Mayo Clinic Platform, a digital health initiative for transforming care delivery at the health facility based in Rochester, Minnesota. The number of data sources is exploding, with Internet of Things (IoT) devices driving a fundamentally new approach to delivering care, especially remote care. Social determinants of health (SDOH) and genomics data are being integrated with data from EHR systems and claim processing systems to gain an increasingly comprehensive understanding of patient populations using advanced analytics and artificial intelligence (AI) tools. Unstructured data, such as clinical notes, is the new goldmine that people are digging into, with the help of emerging technologies such as AI. Obstacles remain. Data interoperability remains a challenge, due in part to the hold proprietary EHR systems have on patient data and the multitude of older applications sitting on disparate databases. Even within health systems, there is a reluctance to freely share data because of political or power reasons. Despite the challenges, Dr. Toby Cosgrove remains enthusiastic. "I am very hopeful and optimistic about the role of technology in providing great healthcare in the future," he says.

Digital transformation requires an enterprise approach to reimagining the business, leveraging technology that is integrated, smart, and intelligent to enable the delivery of care. It is imperative that health systems adopt emerging digital health tools and technologies to enable the shift from "sick care" to prevention and wellness management. For many health systems today, which continue to operate in a margin-constrained fee-for-service model, this poses a conundrum. Preventative healthcare cannibalizes revenue from in-patient hospital stays and other aspects of the traditional healthcare model. Digital transformation inverts the equation between revenue and in-patient stays, as preventative care and population health management take hold and only the sickest need hospitalization, leading to declining in-patient revenues.

In the transition from the current model of healthcare to a new one, declining revenues from traditional sources will likely not be compensated by revenues from new sources, requiring financial commitments in the short term that may not deliver immediate returns. Health systems preparing for the future and considering digital transformation journeys need to start with the question: Do we have a burning platform today? For those that answer no, the question is: Can we sustain indefinitely with our current business model or are we frogs boiling slowly in the water? In the rapidly evolving healthcare marketplace, health systems must carefully consider the major market forces that could impact their future. It is survival of the digital fittest.

The primary forces driving digital transformation, indicated in Figure 1.1, start with the shift from fee-for-service care to value-based care. Though total dollars paid out through

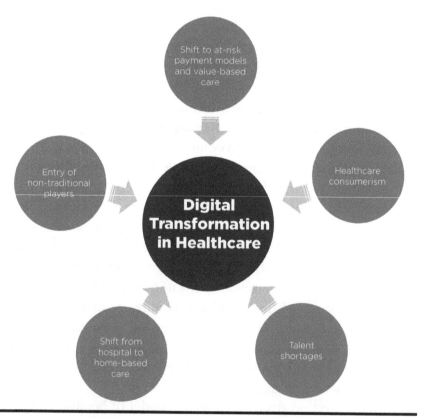

Figure 1.1   Market forces driving digital transformation in healthcare

alternative payment models remain small, nearly two-thirds of insurance payments are tied to some form of value-based care* today. Alongside this shift, newly aware healthcare consumers and a rising cohort of digital natives and millennials are demanding more choice and transparency. Consumers have new expectations around the modalities of healthcare delivery. Almost every cohort of healthcare consumer, from retiring baby boomers to digital-native millennials, is driving the use of technology-enabled care. The older generation requires healthcare to be delivered increasingly at home, while the younger generation demands healthcare services to be provided at a time, place, and modality of their choosing, mostly through a mobile interface. Simplicity is digital nirvana. The explosion of data sources, particularly genomics, wearables, and sensor data, along with advanced analytical capabilities, is driving personalized medicine that will improve outcomes and reduce costs with highly targeted interventions. Declining reimbursement rates will force drastic cost-cutting in the face of margin pressures unless the organization transforms its care delivery models. The time to act is now, while the water is yet to boil.

The terms "digital" and "digitalization" are used interchangeably and often confusingly. Digital refers to technologies that promise to automate and accelerate how a business runs. Digitalization is the integration of digital technologies to reimagine business processes and provide new revenue and value creation opportunities. Digital transformation in healthcare, though a reality, does not have clear definitions. Many leaders are making bold and visionary digital transformation predictions, but few have identified concrete steps to meaningfully actualize the benefits. Through our research, we have

---

* Castellucci, Maria. "Value-Based Health Insurer Contracts Growing in Number, but Not Risk Adoption." *Modern Healthcare News.* August 24, 2019. Accessed December 13, 2019. www.modernhealthcare.com/payment/value-based-health-insurer-contracts-growing-number-not-risk-adoption.

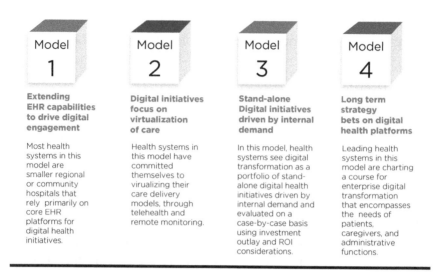

Model 1	Model 2	Model 3	Model 4
Extending EHR capabilities to drive digital engagement	**Digital initiatives focus on virtualization of care**	**Stand-alone Digital initiatives driven by internal demand**	**Long term strategy bets on digital health platforms**
Most health systems in this model are smaller regional or community hospitals that rely primarily on core EHR platforms for digital health initiatives.	Health systems in this model have committed themselves to virualizing their care delivery models, through telehealth and remote monitoring.	In this model, health systems see digital transformation as a portfolio of stand-alone digital health initiatives driven by internal demand and evaluated on a case-by-case basis using investment outlay and ROI considerations.	Leading health systems in this model are charting a course for enterprise digital transformation that encompasses the needs of patients, caregivers, and administrative functions.

Figure 1.2   Digital transformation maturity models in health systems. Source: Damo Consulting Research

identified four stages of maturity in digital transformation efforts in healthcare (Figure 1.2).

Health systems in **Model 1** are focused on maximizing the value of their EHR investments. An example of that is improving patient access through a simple scheduling functionality in an EHR system. Health systems that embrace this model also prefer to rely on their EHR vendor's product roadmap as a guide to their own digital roadmaps.

In **Model 2**, health systems invest in a particular capability such as telehealth and commit to virtualization of care at the departmental or enterprise level. Despite challenges with reimbursement models, telehealth has been effectively deployed for a number of applications by many health systems. Telestroke and virtual visits are widely prevalent applications in telehealth/telemedicine today.

Most health systems have invested in some form of a virtual care model – the most common being telehealth. Various specialties have adapted telehealth models for their practice, and we can now access care through real-time virtual consults, telepsychiatry, teledermatology, and more. Most health systems today have created digital capabilities through smartphone and mHealth applications to improve access to care, manage patient visits to hospitals and clinics, share content to help patients manage their health conditions, engage in secure two-way communication, and improve the overall experience. Increased healthcare consumerism and emerging competition from non-traditional players are among the forces driving this change.

In **Model 3**, health systems address digital transformation by way of a series of stand-alone digital health initiatives that are funded and implemented based on internal demand. However, these digital projects are undertaken mostly in response to near-term priorities and do not necessarily fit into an enterprise digital transformation strategy. Often, the projects are implemented on a suboptimal scale, without consideration for technology standardization across the enterprises, and do not necessarily align with enterprise goals for digital transformation.

Health systems in **Model 4** are developing a comprehensive enterprise-level digital strategy that considers stakeholder priorities across functions and departments. Digital transformation leaders in Model 4 organizations look beyond stand-alone digital health applications. They evaluate strategic information technology (IT) enablers at the infrastructure and application levels needed to support digital health programs, all of which go into securing funding commitments for multi-year digital transformation roadmaps in line with enterprise priorities. Health systems in Model 4 also understand that building an enterprise digital platform requires strategic technology partnerships besides EHR vendors to execute their digital roadmaps.

Today, most systems, especially smaller and mid-tier enterprises, are operating in Models 1 and 2, and larger organizations operate in Models 2 and 3. A handful of leading health systems are in Model 4. Importantly, chief information officers (CIOs) acknowledge that all enterprises need to shift to Model 4, especially if the health system is embracing at-risk payment models. Payment reform is in various stages, depending on the market; however, a large percentage of healthcare reimbursements are going to be at risk for most health systems in the future. Being able to manage care in this context is a significant driver in going beyond incremental initiatives and focusing on developing enterprise-level digital roadmaps. Health systems that take on risks for patient populations also need care coordination across all settings where patients might receive care. For health systems that operate in multiple markets, a key consideration is the regional view in their overall enterprise strategy as there could be important drivers in the regional markets worth recognizing. The mix of patients in a health system often serves to determine to what extent a health system can push the adoption of digital health programs and consequently drive priorities.

A series of focus group discussions* we conducted in the summer of 2019 with nearly 40 CIOs and senior health IT leaders on the current state of digital transformation in healthcare indicate a set of common themes in digital transformation.

Digital transformation is about reimagining business processes and customer experiences. Most CIOs indicate that digital transformation is about using digital technologies to reimagine business processes and customer experiences. In a digital future, this means improving *online* access for patients so that they can get an appointment with their doctor and receive care when they need it. Healthcare leaders also acknowledge the distinction between improving and reimagining business processes; the latter allows for more innovative thinking around delivering care using digital technologies. As an example, healthcare is very local, and the demographics of the populations served are an important part of defining

---

* "The Current State of Healthcare Digital Transformation." Damo Consulting. Accessed December 13, 2019. www.damoconsulting.net/2019/06/30/the-current-state-of-healthcare-digital-transformation-2/.

digital transformation objectives. One executive told us that, in their service area, they serve four generations of patients. For the older generation who still wants to make a phone call, talk to a person, or take a hard copy of their after-visit summary, digital health tools may not be as relevant as they are for younger generations.

The challenge of serving multiple generations is one of many such unique situations requiring digital transformation leaders to reimagine how care should be delivered in the future. Increased competition and reduced reimbursements are also driving health systems to look for ways to work smarter and deliver care more efficiently and effectively. One way to think about it is in terms of reducing friction in workflow processes, such as preventing revenue leakage by developing easy referral processes and implementing them through digital health tools that keep patients within the network.

An emerging theme for digital transformation is also about finding new revenue streams through the monetization of assets and skills. Whether through digital health programs or as part of internal innovation programs, if there is intellectual property or some skill or capability that can be monetized, it becomes part of the mandate for whoever leads the digital transformation function. Many executives who have successfully implemented digital innovation are actively looking at monetizing the applications by offering them to peer systems that are yet to make the investments.

The CIO is also the chief digital officer (CDO), for now. In most health systems, if the board of directors were asked who is responsible for digital initiatives, their response would be the CIO. Most hospitals and health systems in the United States do not have a digital function today. By default, the digital function sits with the CIO in most organizations, even if not formally designated. The lack of a formally designated CDO partly reflects concerns about whether the CDO is another flavor-of-the-month title, like chief integration officer, which was in vogue a few years ago.

Many health systems hesitate to create full-time CDO roles given the current state of maturity of digital transformation in healthcare and lack of appetite to create additional C-level roles. Our focus group CIOs seemed to believe that most health systems are not large enough for two separate roles for CIO and CDO, in sharp contrast to other sectors such as banking that have had full-time CDO roles for a while. IT leaders also struggle to see how the role of CDO is different from the role of a traditional CIO. Many CIOs in our focus group did not see digital initiatives as different from the work they do every day.

The lack of clarity on the role of a CDO may effectively hold back the organization (as well as the CIO) from seizing the opportunities to prepare for the digital future of healthcare. The reality could also be that most health system CIOs are unprepared for CDO roles. Many leading health systems have recruited for this position from outside the industry, bringing in executives who have worked in more digitally mature organizations and have gained valuable knowledge and experience in consumer-facing markets. At the same time, healthcare is unique in that internal customers, such as caregivers, are just as important as external customers (i.e., patients).

An emerging trend among health systems is the setting up of digital transformation offices (DTO), led by a leader with cross-functional influence acting as a strategic enabler for the transformation efforts. The role empowers the digital transformation leader to define roadmaps, identify investment priorities, and facilitate technology partner choices, among others. The DTO also manages the governance processes and reports to the executive leadership and the board on the progress of initiatives and benefits captured from ongoing programs.

Digital budgets are part of IT budgets; however, digital innovation is funded by stakeholders across the enterprise. It would seem logical that digital budgets sit within IT budgets, considering that the chief digital officer role is part of the CIO role in most organizations. However, for most CIOs, it does not matter which budgetary buckets digital investments come out of. At the end of the day, the important question is whether the organization is moving toward digital innovation, and not so much whose budget it is in.

Creative funding models are driving digital investments in many cases. One organization forged a collaboration between its marketing and IT departments to pool their budgets and work together on digital transformation initiatives. Another implemented a project related to automating the provider-credentialing process, the budgets for which came out of the disaster recovery budget because the organization wanted to be able to reproduce records and have backups in case something happened to the paper records. Creative approaches to allocating funds from the capital and operating budgets are also common.

A related question we hear is: How is a digital health project any different from a normal IT project? There is a lack of clarity on this topic among health system CIOs, especially considering that the CDO role is folded into the CIO role. Based on our research, most digital projects typically relate to developing systems of engagement, particularly in relation to patients. Programs such as patient apps and telehealth programs fall into this category. IT infrastructure investments such as LAN/WAN upgrades, unified communications devices, wearables, and sensors may be considered digital health enablers, as would investments in data and analytics environments. Improvements in interoperability and investments in API platforms could completely change the way health systems harness data, exchange information, and accelerate digital innovation.

Most health systems do not have an enterprise digital platform strategy today. The pandemic exposed this gap. As with the definition of digital transformation, the definition of an enterprise digital platform is also emerging. An enterprise digital platform "stack" would include digital experience applications that support digital journeys for a variety of constituents, including patients, caregivers, administrative staff, and the community. Additionally, it would also include infrastructure and the cloud, data integration and management, analytics, and machine learning, among other components. The platform would also require seamless integration with existing and new technologies while remaining scalable and extensible. Many health systems are defaulting to EHR systems as their dominant digital platform strategy and are building around EHR systems or buying digital health point solutions selectively. However, several health systems are also building out their enterprise digital platform stacks in a deliberate and thoughtful way. Regardless of the path toward an enterprise digital platform, all platform strategies need to consider entities beyond the in-patient and ambulatory care facilities and include representation of external entities such as post-acute and community-based care in addition to in-patient care. Above all, the voice of the customer (i.e., the patient) must be represented in the development of digital health experiences.

If we look at the components of an enterprise digital platform as described above, it becomes clear that no single vendor platform meets every need, and health systems must build their own stacks. We will come back to this in Chapters 6 and 7.

Organizational readiness determines the pace of digital transformation. The single biggest barrier to accelerating digital transformation in healthcare today is organizational readiness. As one CIO put it,

> We have major parts of the organization that just are not ready [for transformation] and are clinging to the old ways and will fight us all the way. And that ends up being the majority of the work. The technology is easy. And either you have the budget, or you do not. But it really is getting

the mindsets and the culture moving in the direction you
need to move.

While many digital initiatives are in progress, most healthcare
CIOs in our focus group did not see digital transformation as
a big strategic objective for their organizations (though admit-
tedly, 40 CIOs is not fully representative of the sector as a
whole). When weaving digital innovation into specific initiatives, leaders tend to be overly tactical, looking only at specific
needs at a given time. A related issue is that of organizational
culture and the discipline required to gain agreement on different initiatives, prioritizing the initiatives, and sticking with
the plan. Digital transformation also does not move forward if
an organization is too consumed with other priorities. In one
case, representatives from a health system we spoke with had
just completed an organization-wide migration to a new EHR
platform. The IT department was still reeling from the change,
and their time was almost entirely being consumed with optimizing the new EHR system.

When it comes to digital innovation, CIOs attach high
importance to the level of readiness of the enterprise for
leveraging data and information, including from wearables and
sensors used in delivering care outside of the hospital, and
how that informs the overall care plans for patients. Budget
constraints do seem to play a role, especially in health systems
that face significant ongoing investments just to maintain the
current IT environment and operate the business. From a capital allocation perspective, investments in the business just to
"keep the lights on," which include unavoidable expenses such
as maintaining core platforms including EHR systems, paying wages, and upgrading information security, often use up a
significant portion of available budgets, leaving little room for
transformational activities. Digital initiatives thus need to balance between an immediate or a nearly immediate return on
investment and a long-term view before an enterprise digital
transformation initiative becomes a priority.

How Big Tech Firms and Non-Traditional Players Are Reshaping the Healthcare Market

Given the unsustainable trajectory of healthcare costs in the United States, it comes as no surprise that Karen Murphy, Executive Vice President, Chief Innovation Officer, and the Founding Director of the Steele Institute for Health Innovation at Geisinger, a health system that serves over three million patients in Pennsylvania, states that "The quality of healthcare services we deliver and the price at which we deliver [them] are certainly under scrutiny." As the cost of employer-provided healthcare reaches $20,000* a year for a family of four, Walmart's corporate slogan of "Save Money. Live Better." couldn't be more ironic for the people most impacted by the rising costs of healthcare. It is not surprising then that the company has launched a program[†] to offer a range of healthcare services to Sam's Club members to live up to the corporate slogan. Fed up with healthcare costs consuming an ever-increasing share of operating margins, a group of prominent employers, comprising Berkshire Hathaway, JP Morgan Chase, and Amazon, decided in 2018 to set up a company named Haven Health, headed by well-known physician Dr. Atul Gawande. The primary aim of Haven Health is to reduce healthcare costs for its 1.2 million employees across the sponsor companies.[‡]

---

* Mathews, Anna Wilde. "Cost of Employer-Provided Health Coverage Passes $20,000 a Year." *The Wall Street Journal.* Updated September 25, 2019. Accessed December 24, 2019. www.wsj.com/articles/cost-of-employer-provided-health-c overage-passes-20-000-a-year-11569429000.

† D'Innocenzio, Anne and Tom Murphy. "Walmart's Sam's Club Launches Health Care Pilot to Members." *AP News.* September 26, 2019. Accessed December 13, 2019. https://apnews.com/87286f917cdc440ca5dfc2dfdf0893aa.

‡ Farr, Christina. "Everything We Know About Haven, the Amazon Joint Venture to Revamp Health Care." *CNBC.com.* Updated March 14, 2019. Accessed December 13, 2019. www.cnbc.com/2019/03/13/what-is-haven-amazon-jpmor gan-berkshire-revamp-health-care.html.

Large employers like Amazon and Apple have also separately started offering primary care services to employees through on-campus clinics, while Walmart and CVS have gone the route of providing primary care services through their physical footprint of stores across the nation. Walgreens, at the other end, is trying to build an online relationship with the seven million customers who walk through its stores every day. Even electronics retailer Best Buy* has gotten into the act, declaring its intent to become the chief technology officer (CTO) of our households as remote monitoring devices start pervading our homes. The Geek Squad may soon be part of your care management team.

While it is early days yet, most non-traditional providers of healthcare are targeting a captive audience of employees and consumers. Most healthcare consumers still rely on their traditional provider relationships. As Dr. Toby Cosgrove of Cleveland Clinic puts it,

> There is no question that healthcare is driving increasingly into value. That means keeping costs under control and improving the quality of the care. In parallel, the healthcare system has to improve accessibility since we cannot provide great healthcare unless we have accessible healthcare. I think that technology is going to be a major player in all of these things.

Cosgrove's last point about accessible care has to be seen in the context of the fact that healthcare consumers today are looking for convenience and price transparency in addition to proven and reliable healthcare. Based on this insight, non-traditional healthcare providers such as Walgreens are curating offerings, including from partners, to deliver services ranging from flu shots and lab tests to virtual visits and online second

---

* Wahba, Phil. "Best Buy CEO Explains Her Big Bet on Healthcare Tech." *Fortune*. Accessed December 13, 2019. https://fortune.com/2019/09/26/best-buy-ceo-healthcare-investor-day/.

opinions from renowned healthcare institutions. It was no doubt the same insight that led Walmart to offer a bundle of healthcare services and lower the barriers to care for its Sam's Club members, many of whom were skipping preventative care due to high deductibles.

Digital front door apps (which we discuss in detail in Chapter 2) from non-traditional players are mostly designed to take market share from traditional players by addressing fundamental problems with the way consumers access and pay for care. Over time, the shift may create demand for an entirely new class of healthcare services (Geek Squad for connected health devices?) as adoption rates increase. How does this all play out?

Consumers, especially those who do not feel the need to engage with primary care providers through traditional visits (aka "young invincibles"), will find online/anytime access to care very convenient. The price transparency available for primary and urgent care services through many of these apps may mean that consumers are more likely to avail themselves of these services than a traditional encounter with their primary care physician (PCP).

Traditional health systems, long seen as guilty of delivering poor patient experiences, have upped their game as well. Almost as if in response to a constant barrage of criticism, several major health systems have launched patient apps, offering seamless healthcare experiences to consumers who are looking for convenience as well access to proven and reliable care. By extending the traditional in-person relationship to online and virtual relationships, health systems not only meet the consumer's needs, but can arguably do it much more seamlessly. For instance, an integrated health system running on a single EHR system with standardized workflows is far more likely to deliver a seamless experience compared to stand-alone apps that curate services from several providers whose systems do not talk to each other. That said, many health systems are also participants in the eco-system of partnerships that non-traditional players are creating. We may, therefore, see a future where consumers can access their traditional PCP through multiple access points from different healthcare providers. In the words of Giovanni Monti, Vice President and Director of Healthcare Innovation at Walgreens Boots Alliance, a retail and healthcare giant based in Deerfield, Illinois, with over $130 billion in revenues globally, "The traditional players are also playing their role in non-traditional ways because it is possible today thanks to the evolution of technology, data, interoperability, and regulation to connect the customer and patient journeys in different ways."

Digital health start-ups could be among the biggest gainers in the emerging landscape of online access to care. In the first wave of consumer health apps, most start-ups failed to achieve success with B2C models, realizing that consumers value their physician's advice far too much to take chances with their healthcare. Having switched from B2C to B2B models, start-ups have struggled to navigate the long sales cycles and tortuous path to enterprise adoption for their solutions. Emerging digital front doors from household names like Walgreens and Walmart may overcome consumer doubts and create a pathway to user adoption that could lead to sustainable revenues and growth for some of these start-ups. There are also questions about the efficacy of the solutions. The World Health Organization,* in its recommendations for digital health interventions, has pointed out that amidst the overwhelming proliferation of digital health tools, many digital health solutions are being rolled out without a careful examination of the evidence based on benefits or harms from such

---

* World Health Organization. "WHO Guideline: Recommendations on Digital Interventions for Health System Strengthening." July 10, 2019. www.who.int/pub lications-detail/who-guideline-recommendations-on-digital-interventions-for-heal th-system-strengthening.

solutions. We discuss digital health start-ups and their role in healthcare's digital transformation in Chapter 6 on technology partnerships for digital transformation.

Big tech firms, such as Amazon, Google, Microsoft, and Apple, are making substantial investments in developing cloud-based platforms that they hope will eventually become the backbone of the information system supporting the healthcare sector in a digital future. The pandemic has emboldened their approach. However, it is unlikely that any of the big tech platforms will achieve the winner-take-all dominance they have come to expect and enjoy in sectors such as search optimization and social media platforms. We discuss health cloud platforms in Chapter 6.

There is no doubt that we will see a fundamental shift in the way consumers access healthcare in the future. We will also see access expand significantly to previously underserved populations with the arrival of these new solutions. As David Quirke, CIO of Inova Health System in Northern Virginia, which serves the Washington, DC, metro region, says, "There is a level of inevitability, and frankly, some excitement, in the emergence of these new players in healthcare. From my perspective, I see it as a catalyst to accelerate our ability to deliver quality care."

Notwithstanding the increased competition from non-traditional players, it is likely that we will see an environment where traditional health systems and non-traditional players comfortably coexist as partners and competitors in the future, partnering in the delivery of some areas of care and competing in other areas. Areas where healthcare is behind other sectors, such as designing superior customer experiences, could be the ones where health systems choose to partner with a leading tech firm, such as Apple or Amazon, in the primary care space. However, in delivering high-quality acute care, health systems, especially those with strong brands in their communities, will likely continue to operate on their own and continue to thrive.

Terms such as "ehealth," "mHealth," "big data," and "artificial intelligence" are used synonymously and interchangeably with the term "digital health" today. A useful framework to look at digital health solution areas is shown in Figure 1.3. There is ample indication that most health systems are continuing to invest in virtual care models, including urgent care, e-visits, and video consultations. However, physicians are yet to embrace telemedicine fully and set aside more time for virtual visits because these modalities come with a cost; the reimbursement model for virtual visits is yet to mature, and telehealth visits, by and large, are compensated at lower rates compared to in-person visits.

Tech firms and newer players may operate in an entirely different economic model, one that does not care much for traditional reimbursement models, and this could reshape the healthcare consumer experience in the future. Technology giants like Apple and Amazon, with vast amounts of resources, technology capability, and a deep understanding of consumer

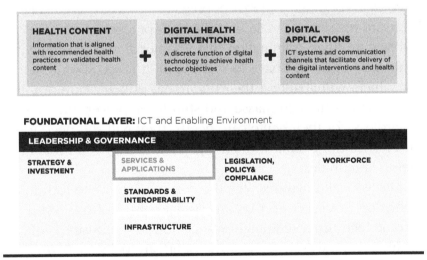

Figure 1.3   Components of digital health. Source: World Health Organization (2019), Creative Commons license*

---

* World Health Organization. *WHO Guideline Recommendations on Digital Interventions for Health System Strengthening.* 2019. Accessed January 27, 2020. www.ncbi.nlm.nih.gov/books/NBK541888/figure/fm-ch1.f2/?report=objectonly.

behavior, are trying to shape an entirely new healthcare experience, piloted and refined within the crucible of a captive healthcare consumer population (i.e., employees). The implication for traditional healthcare firms is that consumers who are redirected from their traditional provider to company-owned and operated clinics for primary care will eventually surrender the ownership of the experience to their employers, who in turn can refine the user experience while providing financial incentives (think Amazon Prime for healthcare). As the focal point of the healthcare consumer experience shifts away from the traditional doctor–patient encounter in a clinic, traditional players will need to come up with ways to retain and strengthen their current relationships.

How serious is this shift and how far can it go? While Apple and Amazon may be able to motivate their employees at their corporate headquarters to shift from their traditional primary care providers to company-owned and operated clinics, they will need a vast network of clinics over time if they have to cover a national or global population of workers. Current licensure restrictions make it difficult to practice medicine across state lines, a limitation that traditional and emerging healthcare firms will have to work with. It is too soon to tell if consumers will abandon their traditional primary care provider relationships en masse and shift to employer-run clinics. Regardless, for their acute care needs, they will still need to turn to health systems with strong brands and deep roots in their communities.

Just as health systems lack the desire or ability to turn into technology enterprises, the same is true of tech firms, even if some tech firms seemingly want to be in the business of healthcare. However, without the right care delivery partnerships, success is far from foretold for technology firms since healthcare experiences are far more personal and carry far higher consequences for consumers (free return shipping is of no use for a poor healthcare experience). For their part, health systems that are at risk of losing control over the primary care experience will need to find ways to remain the preferred destination for acute and in-patient care. We have seen some version of this play out in the health insurance sector, with employers increasingly underwriting medical costs and retaining the services of insurers for administrative services.

Healthcare is a large industry with plenty of room for companies – incumbents, innovators, and start-ups – who are making significant investments to bring technology-enabled innovation to healthcare. The fundamentals of healthcare have not changed; it is still about the highly personal interaction between a patient and a trained and empathic physician or caregiver, regardless of whether the experience is enabled through a digital front door or a real one. With convenience and price transparency being the new rules of the game, more participants get a chance to reimagine this experience for the future.

In the coming years, innovative partnerships, sometimes between traditional competitors, will redefine the healthcare industry as we know it. In 2018, CVS and Aetna merged to form a healthcare behemoth with nearly $195 billion in revenues.* The same year, insurance major Cigna acquired the PBM company Express Scripts,[†] gaining significant leverage in negotiating the price of drugs. Large employers, alarmed at the rising costs of healthcare, are looking to regain control over how their employees can be managed to improve overall health and avoid medical costs. Health systems continue to consolidate rapidly to maintain negotiating power against the concentration of purchasing power among a handful of large insurers. Along with a steady shift of control of employee health and

---

* Health, CVS. 2019. "Millennials have the world at their fingertips but it's harming their health, CVS Health study finds." July 29. Accessed December 13, 2019. https://cvshealth.com/newsroom/press-releases/millennials-have-world-their-fingertips-its-harming-their-health-cvs-health.

[†] "Cigna Completes Combination with Express Scripts, Establishing a Blueprint to Transform the Health Care System." Cigna. Accessed December 13, 2019. https://www.cigna.com/newsroom/news-releases/2018/cigna-completes-combination-with-express-scripts-establishing-a-blueprint-to-transform-the-health-care-system.

wellness management toward their employers, we are witnessing a perfect storm that could fundamentally alter the current healthcare landscape and the relationships between providers and patients. Tech firms such as Apple and Google are making significant investments in building technology solutions, partnering with health systems, and investing in data acquisition on a large scale. Companies that came into existence in the 21st century, such as Facebook, Uber, and Lyft, are competing with giants from the previous era in staking out a claim on the healthcare sector's 3.6 trillion dollars at play.*

With giant corporations betting big on healthcare, we have to ask what is behind it all. The answer is simple: ownership of the healthcare consumer experience and, by extension, the consumer. Taking a cue from the markets, many health systems are investing in digitalizing their relationships with consumers.

How Leading Health Systems Are Approaching Digital Health

"Digital medicine is just medicine in the same way that really good technology is not about technology," says Daniel Barchi, Senior Vice President and CIO of New York Presbyterian Hospitals. "It blends into the fabric of what we do in our everyday lives."

Even prior to the pandemic, virtual visits and e-visits are commonplace in healthcare. A young mother of three no longer has to bundle her kids into the car and drive an hour each way to her hospital for a routine follow-up that takes all of 15 minutes in the physician's office. A senior citizen in a wheelchair on multiple chronic care medications no longer needs to

---

* "National Health Expenditure Data: Historical." CMS.gov. Accessed December 13, 2019. www.cms.gov/Research-Statistics-Data-and-Systems/Statistics-Trends-and-Reports/NationalHealthExpendData/NationalHealthAccountsHistorical.

physically check-in at a physician's office. Aging veterans find it increasingly challenging to drive hundreds of miles for care. They can all do their visits through secure messaging or, if required, through a virtual real-time consultation. In between, the hospital can remotely monitor patients, ready to intervene with a home visit if necessary.

While healthcare shifts away from in-patient stays, we are likely to see more procedures carried out in outpatient facilities. At the same time, we are going to see the acuity of patients who end up in the hospital go up more and more. We are also seeing less acute disease and more chronic disease in the population at large, and chronic disease is going to be managed more in the home and physician's office as opposed to a hospital setting. As healthcare shifts from the hospital and clinic to home-based care, traditional health systems have a significant advantage over emerging players when it comes to understanding their patient populations and serving them better. At Geisinger Health in Pennsylvania, a pilot program* to bring care to the homes of older patients with complex healthcare needs delivered a 35 percent drop in emergency department visits, a 40 percent decline in hospital admissions, and an average annual reduction in spending per patient of almost $8,000. Technology is enabling patient-generated health data from wearables and sensors that include blood pressure, heart rate, glucose levels, and medication adherence to be transmitted seamlessly into the patient's electronic medical record. The combined data is analyzed for trends and insights and made available to everyone involved in that patient's care, enabling care teams to manage the patient more effectively. Geisinger analyzed data from traditional EHR systems as well as claims data and social determinants to identify patients most at risk and deliver comprehensive care using a team of caregivers.

---

* Tomcavage, J. F., Ryu, J., and Doddamani, S. "Geisinger's Home Care Program is Cutting Costs and Improving Outcomes." *Harvard Business Review.* November 6, 2019. https://hbr.org/2019/11/geisingers-home-care-program-is-cutting-costs-and-improving-outcomes.

Data-driven advancements are arriving in the form of precision medicine and healthcare consumerism. Advancements in precision medicine are expected as the relationship between data from wearables, sensors, social determinants, and other emerging sources is better interpreted through advanced AI and yields better outcomes. We are in the early stages of a new push toward patient-centered, consumer-directed care. As care delivery shifts more toward remote or outpatient settings, the care protocols and treatments are going to continue to get more sophisticated and increasingly augmented by the technologies that are now emerging.

We are also starting to see some redistribution of in-person visits between traditional providers and emerging ones. As an example, CVS and Aetna are betting that consumers will prefer to visit one of their many walk-in clinics for minor conditions instead of waiting to schedule an appointment with their primary care physician at the hospital down the road. Urgent care is already shifting out of hospitals and, in many cases, going virtual altogether. The rise of companies such as Teladoc and Doctor on Demand is clear evidence of this. None of this suggests that the traditional healthcare setting is fading into obscurity.

Health systems, especially those with strong brands in their local and regional markets, have an unassailable lead today as trusted healthcare partners in their communities. Many of them are already making big investments in digitalization programs that will enable consumers to get the best of both worlds, namely, a virtual experience for routine healthcare and urgent care needs, and an in-patient experience for acute care needs. For a high-quality patient journey, these two worlds must be tightly integrated. Only traditional hospitals can provide that truly integrated experience today.

Ownership of the healthcare consumer experience requires a mixture of convenience and quality enabled by robust data and analytics capability. No healthcare provider sits precisely at that happy intersection today. However, the race is already underway to get there. If the relationship between big data and precision medicine has been on a more or less predictable trajectory, the explosive growth of healthcare consumerism has opened up options for healthcare consumers seeking convenience in addition to quality care. The healthcare leaders of tomorrow will ideally balance these two critical aspects of healthcare delivery. A reputation built on high-quality care alone will no longer be enough; neither will a reputation for slick user interfaces and transactional convenience.

The biggest unknown in the emerging scenarios is the evolution of healthcare consumer preferences. Indications are that consumers are getting more comfortable with digital health technologies driven by data from the growing use of remote monitoring devices, wearables, and the like. We do not think twice about getting our prescriptions filled electronically anymore, and we are increasingly trawling the web for medical information. However, we are still in the early stages of a definite shift toward virtual care, and big concerns around privacy violations arising from unfettered access to patient medical information by some big tech firms are yet to be overcome. However, some firms appear to enjoy the trust of healthcare providers and consumers alike. Apple has built collaborative networks with over a hundred leading health systems for data sharing and delivering personalized health experiences via digital health apps on the iPhone.

Digital transformation is not just about patients and consumers. It is also about how to improve the experience for clinicians, nursing staff, administrators, researchers, educators, students, and other members of the overall workforce in a health system. Nader Mherabi, CIO of NYU Langone Health in New York City, has over 30 years of experience in the information technology field and has implemented large-scale systems for top Fortune 500 companies worldwide. He is cautious about the focus on patient experience at the cost of other priorities. He insists, "We don't want to improve the experience for patients and families at the expense of the clinicians."

In other words, we need to meet the needs of providers to meet the needs of patients.

The technology that is important for digital health blends seamlessly into what caregivers do daily without getting in their way while they take care of patients. Importantly, the technology must not take up additional physician or nurse time at the expense of time spent on patient care. Cultural factors often play a role in the effectiveness of digital solutions. As an example, even with core EMR systems that have very good patient portals, few health systems have really made inroads in getting their patients to use them. And even when the functionality exists, getting the physicians and physician practices to use them can be challenging. Something as simple as allowing access to a physician's calendar for scheduling patient visits can be fraught with challenges because many physicians are reluctant to share access. They like control over their schedules and understanding exactly which patients are getting scheduled and when. The fact is that healthcare as an industry is new to a digital way of working. Most health systems are using very low thresholds to measure progress with digital practices and are focused mostly on usage levels, which is indicative of the level of digital maturity for the sector as a whole.

The basic challenge for digital transformation leaders is to answer questions such as: How does the new technology tool work for the end user? Can we cut down the time that they spend on technology by making it more passive and ubiquitous? How do we reduce friction at the human–technology interface? The answers to many of these questions are determined by the people and the process side of digital transformation, and less on the technology itself.

While we see the top tier health systems put real dollars behind digital transformation, the urgency to act is not as visible in the next tier of health systems such as regional or community hospitals, which could benefit from digital enablement in driving care delivery efficiencies and improved outcomes. We recognize that not every hospital in the country has the

ability or the financial resources for another large-scale technology-led transformation after the significant investments in
electronic health record systems in the last decade. Our position is that health systems that are not embracing digital transformation and digital health could be at risk of losing their
place in the future state of the healthcare system.

There is also a level of hype in the marketplace related
to all things digital. Most healthcare enterprises and solution
providers look at digital in a narrow context, such as improving access, and even within that context, it is often a certain
aspect, such as scheduling, that may be digitalized, with all
other aspects of the patient journey being the same as before
(i.e., a manual or in-person experience). For digital transformation to fulfill its promise, the delivery of healthcare services
has to resemble the seamlessness of an Amazon experience,
from placing the order to its packing, shipping, tracking, and
delivery. In the healthcare context, due to a patchwork of
systems and broken processes, solutions are often stand-alone,
unconnected systems. Even within a single health system,
caregivers may work with more than one EHR system when
serving a patient's complete needs over the care cycle. These
experiences may look like digital from the outside, but under
the covers, the fragmentation of workflow and systems creates
more work, increases costs, and impacts the patient experience and quality of care.

So, what is holding back digital transformation efforts?
Based on our observations across health systems, there are
several factors that influence the adoption of digital health:
financial resources, technology capabilities, and multiple competing priorities are some of these factors. However, there are
a handful of cultural factors that effectively hold back healthcare organizations from making rapid progress. As with all
transformational pursuits, the biggest obstacle to success is not
technology. It is not lack of vision. It is culture, every time.

We refer to cultural barriers as **the enemy within**. It
all starts with clarity at the top. The CEO needs to not only

provide absolute clarity in identifying and defining the role of the digital transformation leader, but also ensure that the executive team plays well together. Attempting digital transformation requires unity of command, accountability, and transparency. We understand this sounds like a consultant sound bite, but we speak from real experience.

With several emerging roles and titles in healthcare organizations, it is not uncommon to encounter misalignment between a CIO and roles such as chief digital officer, chief innovation officer, and chief patient experience officer. Prior to the "digital" era, technology ownership was clearly in the hands of the CIO. Few leaders outside of IT understood technology. The boundaries were abundantly clear. Swim lanes were not required. The democratization of access to application development tools and cloud-based software-as-a-service has blurred the lines between traditional and emerging IT experts, a phenomenon referred to as bi-modal or two-speed IT. **Everyone is an expert**, or at least they think they are. In fact, some may know more than your CIO. In the past, nobody had the knowledge to challenge the CIO. Today everyone can, to some degree. While diversity of opinion is key to formulating best decisions, having every leader opine on digital transformation will slow down progress at the organizational level.

Given the hyper focus on digital transformation, **everyone wants to lead**. Conflicting priorities emerge. Politics ensue. Bureaucracy accelerates. Digital adoption slows. Colleagues/ departments all have their own favorite vendors and priorities. With conflicting ideas about what digital could and should do for the organization, chaos ensues. A year may pass, and digital transformation remains a theory. Nothing will short-circuit your digital transformation faster than infighting on your team.

The bottom line is that organizations that have the sponsorship for digital transformation at the highest levels, that have identified and clearly articulated their top four or five initiatives, and that have created an organizational model with role clarity and accountability are the ones that are making the most progress with digital transformation for the future. We discuss the importance of organization models and best practices in Chapter 7.

Key Takeaways and Action Steps

1. Digital transformation is about reimagining business processes and online customer experiences. Most health systems fall in one of four maturity states described in this chapter regarding digital transformation.
2. In the face of unsustainable costs and a permanent shift to telehealth models, health systems must invest in virtual care technologies to transform the way care is delivered in the future.
3. Non-traditional players such as CVS Health, Walgreens, and Walmart are reshaping the healthcare market. Big tech firms, which include Amazon, Google, Microsoft, and Apple, are making substantial investments in developing the digital health platforms of the future.
4. A shift toward the virtualization of healthcare, vast amounts of venture capital pouring into digital health, and new data sources are driving digital health innovation and healthcare outcomes.
5. Health systems must start with online consumer experiences and develop a comprehensive enterprise-level digital strategy that considers stakeholder priorities across functions and departments. Digital transformation requires using technology that is integrated, smart, and intelligent to enable the delivery of care.
6. Organizational readiness determines the pace of digital transformation. Health systems need to balance between an immediate or a nearly immediate return on investment and a long-term view on enterprise digital transformation.

7. Retreat idea: Convene a digital transformation retreat with your team and bring in an external facilitator to do an environment assessment. Ask questions such as: Who are our competitors? What are leading health systems doing in digital transformation? What are the best practices with digital in other industries? How are your strategic technology partners positioned to support you in your digital journey?

8. What gaps has the COVID-19 pandemic exposed that we need to address or reconsider?

THIRTY-SECOND AGILE CONSULT

Where on the digital maturity model (Figure 1.2) do you see your organization today, and where do you expect to be in 12 months?

Chapter 2

The Future of
Digital Health

Health systems desire innovative technology-enabled solutions
that can improve patient and caregiver experiences. Healthcare
has traditionally followed other sectors when it comes to
technology adoption. Most health systems are not set up to
innovate on a large scale. However, the COVID-19 pandemic
has put healthcare on an accelerated path to transformation.
Being a fast follower enables healthcare organizations to adopt
proven solutions quickly without taking on too much technology risk. As we look to the future of digital health, we look at
five major areas of emphasis:

1. Enabling online patient experiences
2. Improving caregiver experiences
3. Digitally enabling administrative functions
4. Enhancing wellness in our communities
5. Creating new lines of revenue

Enabling Online Patient Experiences: Telehealth and Digital Front Doors

"Our mission is to move our relationships with consumers from an offline relationship to an online relationship," declares Aaron Martin, Chief Digital Officer of Seattle-based Providence Health, a health system with nearly 120,000 employees serving patients across six states. Martin, who was General Manager of Amazon's self-publishing and print-on-demand business prior to joining Providence Health, is on a mission to put the focus back on patients, improve engagement levels to achieve better healthcare outcomes, and reduce costs.

Digital has become the price of entry into healthcare's future state and a powerful tool for differentiation in the healthcare experience of the future. However, digital itself is not a strategy but an enabler of an overall strategy and a tool to unlock value. The digital front door is a means to digitally engage patients at major touchpoints of the patient journey and leverages multiple technologies to increase patient access, drive higher patient satisfaction and increased revenue. An overall digital strategy can be a combination of approaches depending on the strategic goals of the company.

"Consumers have two types of relationships with healthcare providers: the transactional and the agency," says John Glaser. Glaser is a former CIO of Boston-based Partners Healthcare, one of the largest health systems in the country, with over $13 billion in revenues in 2018. As Glaser notes, something is afoot in the world of transactional healthcare. A raft of new solutions has hit the market, aimed at capturing the first point of contact with consumers in need of healthcare services. These solutions are now broadly referred to as "digital front doors." An example of a digital front door is the digital marketplace app launched by Walgreens, named Find Care,* which offers a

---

* "Find Care." Walgreens. Accessed December 13, 2019. https://news.walgreens.co m/press-releases/general-news/walgreens-introduces-new-digital-marketplace-featuring-17-leading-health-care-providers.htm.

slew of healthcare services, from lab tests to virtual consults. Many of these services are provided by the dozens of partners featured on the portal that include digital health companies, such as MDLIVE and Propeller Health, and traditional healthcare providers, such as Advocate Aurora Health and LabCorp. In most cases, prices are listed for the services.

The Walgreens app is symbolic of a significant shift in how consumers gain access to care. Traditional providers have long faced the challenge of access; the issues range from multiple points of access to inadequate and lack of timely access. A lack of proper access leads to an immediate loss of revenue as well as the risk of an improper match between patient and provider.

Graham Gardner, MD, is the founder and CEO of Kyruus, a routing and scheduling platform for health systems that helps to ensure that patients within its network are getting to the right network provider. Gardner likens his company's approach to the tactics described in *Moneyball*, the famous book by Michael Lewis about the Oakland Athletics who dramatically improved their performance using statistical analysis under coach Billy Beane (played by Brad Pitt in the movie adaptation). Kyruus, which has raised significant amounts of venture capital funding, was founded on the idea that it's possible to use statistics to understand the relative competencies of physicians and use that information to put them "up to bat" in situations where they're more likely to do well. Dr. Gardner began with the assumption that physicians were operating the same way as ballplayers, trying to hit every pitch (i.e., help every patient). And yet, statistically, there are huge variations in the cost and quality of care resulting from this scattershot approach.

With a more granular view of providers and their specialties, Kyruus uses statistics to understand what a doctor might be best suited to treat and matches them with the right kinds of patients, a task that is further complicated by the ever-increasing specialization in medical practice. As Dr. Gardner points out, "Instead of the go-to ortho guy that I would normally send all my orthopedic cases to, there is now a hand person, an elbow person, foot and ankle, spine, et cetera."

The bottom line is that health systems are struggling to match supply and demand at scale, and patients are waiting far too long to access care. As a result, patients are either not getting the care they need from the provider they want or are leaking out of the network and seeking care elsewhere. The latter is more disturbing for providers today. The discontinuity created by poor patient access is an opportunity for emerging non-traditional providers to win consumers away. Once consumers have switched modes to a new way of accessing care, traditional providers have all but lost control of the primary care experience and may become reliant on the new merchants of healthcare consumerism.

At Inova Health in northern Virginia, CIO David Quirke likes to think in terms of reimagining primary care and breaking down the patient journey in a "lean-like" model. His approach to digital front doors is to understand the touchpoints of primary care delivery, from arrival to rooming, ordering results, and managing the post-visit experience. Rather than looking at a specific technology and how to deploy it, he prefers to think through how Inova wants a given experience to be for its patients and caregivers and how a technology can enable that. Quirke offers geolocation technology as an example of how healthcare providers can change the way they welcome and greet patients by "spotting" the patients when they enter a hospital facility. For Quirke, one important consideration is equipping caregivers with the right technology tools. He is looking at technologies such as voice recognition, where the EHR becomes a vital but more passive element of the experience, enabling physicians to provide better care by using a voice-enabled interface to reduce the time spent on activities such as scribing. Ultimately, he wants to make sure that the technologies Inova Health is deploying facilitate a much smoother experience for both the patient and the caregiver.

Other non-traditional players are developing alternatives for primary care access. CVS Health, a giant healthcare company that emerged from the merger of retail pharmaceutical chain CVS and insurance major Aetna, has launched a series of HealthHUBs* in its walk-in clinics (which it refers to as the new front doors for healthcare), where patient navigators steer healthcare consumers to a series of available services, including in-person consultations with primary care physicians in the store. While this doesn't sound at first like a digital front door, consider this: Having access to the combined patient health records of CVS and Aetna means that their consumers' healthcare records can be analyzed and their needs and care gaps identified, enabling caregivers to proactively reach out and schedule services such as routine visits, prescription refills, or periodic tests.

Many leading healthcare providers have risen to the challenge. Carolinas-based Atrium Health has launched a digital front door† where patients can look up their symptoms in a symptom tracker, decide how they want to access care (virtual, e-visit, or urgent care), and review prices for the various options. Atrium Health has also pioneered the use of voice-enabled healthcare services‡ based on Amazon Alexa. Washington-based Providence Health and Illinois-based Advocate Aurora Health have launched chatbot services that work as symptom triage tools, helping consumers analyze their symptoms through a bot interface and directing them to their care options.

Many health systems have invested in telehealth capabilities covering routine consultations as well as online urgent care.

---

* Tully, Shawn. "CVS Wants to Make Your Drugstore Your Doctor." Fortune. May 17, 2019. Accessed December 13, 2019. https://fortune.com/longform/cvs-aetna-health-care/.

† "Get Care Now." Atrium Health. Accessed December 13, 2019. https://atriumhealth.org/medical-services/get-care-now.

‡ "Alexa, Find the Nearest Atrium Health Urgent Care." Atrium Health. April 8, 2019. Accessed December 13, 2019. https://atriumhealth.org/about-us/newsroom/news/2019/04/atrium-health-patients-can-now-use-amazons-alexa.

Teledermatology, telepsychiatry, and telestroke are becoming increasingly mainstream. These capabilities are somewhat different from the kind of digital front door experiences that consumers need today (setting aside digital marketing efforts to raise awareness and drive inbound inquiries, which fall outside the purview of care delivery). Consumers need help figuring out what their symptoms could mean, which helps avoid the effort and delays in getting through to the right provider for advice. Today, most consumers rely on "Dr. Google" for medical information online – not exactly the recommended standard of care.

The reimagining of the primary care experience needs to go well beyond implementing virtual health tools and hoping that consumers will start using them. Today's consumers need instant access to information and immediate fulfillment of care needs. In the post COVID-19 era, consumers used to the human experience of a doctor–patient interaction are getting used to an online and remote version of that experience. Traditional and emerging providers of primary care services must find ways to meet these expectations. Aaron Martin of Providence Health says, "As an industry, we need to be transaction ready. That means we must collectively build infrastructure with which we can send, receive, and book any resource and be able to move information around."

Deep personalization and localization are becoming the bare minimum required for healthcare providers as dissatisfaction with the status quo takes hold and consumers start to seek alternatives to traditional healthcare relationships. We have seen this play out in other sectors, notably the retail, banking, and securities markets. However, there is a big difference in healthcare. The fact that healthcare data is not easily portable from one provider to another is a significant challenge for consumers looking to transition between providers seamlessly. Engaging with multiple providers comes with downsides in the form of discontinuities in the longitudinal medical records of patients. Big tech firms, notably Apple, are trying to address this gap through a comprehensive approach to building a new healthcare technology infrastructure that ensures that records are not only complete and current, but also accessible to the consumers to whom they belong.

There is a huge opportunity now for the likes of CVS Health and Walgreens to disrupt the status quo and win over disaffected healthcare consumers. Health systems have no option but to change the status quo and embrace virtual care models. the experience in other sectors is anything to go by, healthcare enterprises that do not embrace digital are a hair's breadth away from seeing their most cherished relationships disrupted forever.

Notwithstanding the changes afoot in the world of transactional healthcare, the story is different in the world of agency relationships between the healthcare consumer and the traditional healthcare provider. The strong bonds between consumers and their trusted physicians cannot be easily replaced, meaning health systems with strong brands and community connections are still the preferred choice for acute care. Having a strong brand also puts traditional health systems in a position to expand their healthcare services beyond acute care and serve additional consumer needs such as wellness, preventative care, and routine primary care. Many health systems are aggressively expanding into the primary care space by acquiring physician practices. Their strategy is to enhance scale economies and negotiating power with payers through growth. This includes adding outpatient posts while simultaneously engaging in mergers and acquisitions. As David Quirke says, "I think successful organizations will always put patients and quality first, and everything else follows."

Improving Caregiver Experiences: Beyond EHR

A study published by the Mayo Clinic noted that the 870 US physicians surveyed graded the usability of EHR systems at an F,* confirming the long-standing view of the clinical community that EHR systems are a big burden on providers of care. Complaints about the burden of EHR systems include the loss of ability to maintain sufficient eye contact with patients as physicians hunch over their laptops to document the encounter, "pajama time" doing after-hours work, completing visit summaries, the burnout epidemic, and medical errors that can cause serious patient harm. An oft-quoted goal of digital transformation today is to bring joy back to the practice of medicine.

EHR systems are the de facto operating systems for digital health today. Since the Affordable Care Act (ACA) and the Health Information Technology for Economic and Clinical Health (HITECH) Act were passed over a decade ago, there is now near-total penetration of EHR systems in the provider space. This was accomplished in no small measure, with over $30 billion in federally funded Meaningful Use incentives that went toward helping hospitals and physician practices pay for the cost of implementing the systems.† In the process, a handful of EHR vendors – notably Epic and Cerner – have gained dominant market positions, accounting for a majority of EHR system installations. Our research shows that a significant portion of current IT budgets is consumed by EHR platforms, mainly for optimizing and upgrading the existing installations. This is one of the reasons digital transformation in healthcare has been slow. The price of maintaining these applications remains egregious. Many health systems are also looking to EHR platforms as the default choice for their digital initiatives

---

* Melnick, Edward R., Liselotte N. Dyrbye, Christine A. Sinsky, Mickey Trockel, Colin P. West. 2019. "The Association Between Perceived Electronic Health Record Usability and Professional Burnout Among US Physicians." *Mayo Clinic Proceedings*, November 14, 476–487. https://doi.org/10.1016/j.mayocp.2019.09.024.
† "Data and Program Reports." CMS.gov. Accessed December 13, 2019. www.cms.gov/Regulations-and-Guidance/Legislation/EHRIncentivePrograms/DataAndReports.

whenever a certain functionality is available. However, EHR platforms may not be the ideal platforms for driving healthcare's digital future. We are entering a phase in healthcare when technology is advancing very quickly and no one company can service all of the needs of the healthcare system.

For their part, EHR vendors are working to improve their products and seize the opportunities of healthcare's digital transformation to maintain their dominant positions. Sean Bina, Vice President of Patient Experience with Epic Systems, points out:

> Twenty years ago, the world was very different in terms of what was available from a digital perspective. There were not integrated ambulatory inpatient solutions, and you could not do an end-to-end revenue cycle that covered all of your hospitals and clinics. And so, people were trying to cobble together best-of-breed systems to manage all of it. Until around 2003, there was not even such a thing as a patient portal. I think it is important to remember how far we have come. Now we have fully integrated systems that cover all the food, warmth, and shelter needs of healthcare organizations. We are just now getting to the point where we can do a little bit more of the poetry.

As a result of the widespread adoption of standardized EHR systems that have replaced siloed stand-alone systems, we're now starting to see physicians go from thinking of patient records as a collection of disparate data points to wanting to have combined digital views of all of a patient's information pulled seamlessly together. In fact, healthcare has moved beyond looking at isolated patient charts to a seamless and continuous healthcare experience enabled by information technology. This is what we mean by digital health.

There is a growing expectation that healthcare organizations are going to be able to take inputs from a variety of sources, pull them all together, and make diagnosis and treatment decisions that improve the quality of care. Notably, this will bring us closer to experiencing precision medicine. Health systems need to balance all their technology investments to ensure the organization is well positioned for the future. This may mean leveraging EHR to manage core healthcare operations. However, healthcare organizations are also looking closely at going beyond EHR vendors to partner selectively with emerging digital health start-ups and major technology companies for capabilities such as advanced analytics and AI, digital consumer experiences, and cloud hosting. With improved interoperability between proprietary IT systems, this approach not only allows healthcare enterprises to take advantage of best-in-class capabilities from the broader technology ecosystem, but also mitigates risks that arise from overreliance on a single dominant vendor.

Digitally Enabling Administrative Functions: Automation

While digital health innovators and healthcare executives are focused on front-end applications that drive revenue and patient satisfaction, they often lose sight of the fact that some of the biggest opportunities for digital transformation lie in improving organization efficiencies, especially in administrative functions. Healthcare is a labor-intensive sector, and the industry expects continuing labor shortages for the extended future. One way to address labor shortages is through the use of automation technologies, especially robotic process automation (RPA). RPA can take on mundane and repetitive tasks and release human resources to more value-added activities.

Many health systems have successfully deployed RPA tools in backend functions such as revenue cycle management, often overlaying AI tools to predict certain outcomes, such as a claim rejection. Human resource functions have automated the initial screening of employment applications using similar tools. Automation tools can perform many of the paralegal functions in an enterprise. Digital workplace collaboration tools have significantly improved employee efficiency while increasing the quality of work and raising workplace satisfaction scores. Digital collaboration platforms are bringing about a step change in supply operations, reducing overheads and costs that flow straight to the bottom line. In an effort to reduce physician burdens, many health systems are exploring automation tools for activities such as scribing and documentation.

Seth Hain, Vice President of Research and Development at Epic Systems in charge of the company's advanced analytics programs, sees real opportunities for automation, using machine learning to save time and energy moving patients through operational workflows. An interesting example of improving administrative efficiencies is identifying – and reducing – no-shows. Using automation tools and analytics, patients who are most likely to be no-shows can be nudged with a reminder phone call or text informing them that they are due for the appointment. The tools can also identify the patients who are at the highest risk and need to get in the soonest, prioritizing such patients automatically when new appointments become available. These approaches not only improve the convenience and access for patients, but also help the healthcare organization fill otherwise empty time slots, creating win-win outcomes.

Many other creative uses of automation and robotics are emerging. At New York–Presbyterian Hospital, an intelligent robot carries food from the basement kitchens to patient rooms so that the kitchen staff can focus on food preparation. The robot can press a button on the elevator to get to the destination floor where a human caregiver receives the food and delivers it personally to patients.

As RPA tools become more intelligent through continuous learning, they will be able to reduce administrative workloads on routine tasks and take on more intelligent ones. Health systems must not only take advantage of the labor-saving benefits of such tools, but also carefully evaluate the workforce needs of the future and ensure that employees are reskilled and trained appropriately in anticipation of a future where many bots will indeed replace humans.

Enhancing Wellness in Our Communities: Population Health Management

Most health systems' mission or vision statements include references to improving the well-being of their local communities There are several factors that motivate health systems in helping keep populations healthy in an era of accountable care. Influenced by a combination of community benefit political requirements and natural altruism, all organizations care deeply about the communities they serve. Even in the smallest of hospitals, someone has the task of ensuring strong community relations. This often comes in the form of being an active participant, if not a leader, in municipal health-oriented programs.

Another factor influencing how health systems approach community wellness is the shift toward a capitated reimbursement model, where a flat fee is paid for every patient, regardless of what it takes to treat them or keep them healthy. The trend is one of the primary drivers behind the emergence of new care models such as accountable care organizations. As we continue to move from a fee-for-service model to value-based care models, population health management becomes an important discipline in keeping patients healthy and keeping them out of hospitals. The digitalization of care delivery processes and the use of advanced analytics for risk profiling and stratification of patient populations will be a requirement for solvency and sustainability for many healthcare organizations in future. With more financial risk shifting to providers, we can no longer ignore the changing economics of healthcare. Health systems will not survive without it.

It is widely established that health systems and care providers can only influence roughly 20 percent of a person's wellbeing. The other 80 percent comes down to individual choices and social determinants of health. Health systems must be cautious in allocating resources to materially impact this 20 percent while figuring out ways to influence the remaining 80 percent. Evidence-based programs powered by digital interventions can make a difference in community wellness. Several health systems, including CommonSpirit Health, Kaiser Permanente, Geisinger, and MetroHealth, are showing early yet promising results.

The healthcare model is shifting from standard treatment protocols for "sick care" to prevention and personalized medicine. As health systems engage with patients, the focus should not only be about the convenience of access; we also need to encourage healthy habits such as fitness and eating well, reaching patients before they ever need chronic or acute health services. Several leading healthcare organizations are doing just that. UnitedHealthcare* incentivizes employees with programs that monitor their fitness. For example, if a participant averages over 10,000 steps per day, they receive a monetary award of $1.25 daily. Cleveland Clinic has seen its employee benefit costs reduce by launching a similar program. Employees can also reduce their health insurance costs based on activity data they share with benefit administrators.

When managing populations, health systems can use data analytics and AI to identify and proactively reach out to patients. Simple examples include the ability to identify

---

* Gartenberg, Chaim. *UnitedHealthcare Adds the Apple Watch to Its Fitness-Tracking Reward Program*. March 7, 2018. Accessed January 29, 2020. https://newsroom.uhc.com/experience/apple-watch-rewards.html.

all patients due for a routine physical test or mammogram. Complex examples include the ability to predict which patients might eventually require invasive cardiovascular care unless intervention takes place. Using such data, administrators can reach out to their respective populations and ensure they receive the care they need.

A significant number of digital health start-ups focus on helping individuals manage their wellness with the help of intuitive and engaging apps. Fitness and nutrition-tracking apps are common, as are sleep-tracking and meditation apps. Start-ups are increasingly addressing very specific population needs, such as women's health, teen health, senior care, and so on. Apple's Health app is an example of digital technology that enables individuals to track and manage their health and wellness, combining their personal activity data with their medical histories that are pulled from their healthcare provider's EHR systems. Google's acquisition of Fitbit is another example of how the industry focus is shifting in this direction. As home-monitoring technologies further integrate with wearable devices, we will see a convergence of technology solutions that increasingly enable patients to receive healthcare within their homes or on the move and enable caregivers to track their health and wellness remotely and intervene as necessary.

Creating New Lines of Revenue: Monetizing Digital Platforms

To remain solvent, health systems must not only embrace and exploit digital transformation, but also leverage these new platforms to create new lines of business. Financially sustaining health systems on patient care reimbursements alone will not suffice. Leading systems are already leveraging their digital transformation investments to generate additional sources of income. As tech companies and non-traditional players enter traditional healthcare markets, health systems must diversify to compete.

As health systems create and advance their platforms, monetization opportunities are numerous. A caveat: while the revenues from each of these individual initiatives described may not create significant revenues in the broad context of a healthcare delivery enterprise, these incremental revenue streams nevertheless add to the bottom line in the short term and have the potential to become significant money-makers at some point in future.

Data and Analytics Platform

The oft-quoted Murphy's golden rule says, "whoever has the gold makes the rules." The metaphorical gold in this case is healthcare data. As digital health innovators and healthcare enterprises alike try to improve access, convenience, and outcomes for consumers, data is front and center in how health systems are transforming themselves for the competitive landscape of the future. As traditional healthcare enterprises confront emerging competition from non-traditional players, some of them have started appreciating the competitive advantage of their data on healthcare consumers' medical histories.

A health system that has a solid data analytics platform capable of managing population health could consider selling this service as a platform to another system, creating a sustainable recurring revenue stream. A hospital that is considering making a data analytics purchase from a tech company, where there might be some trust issues, can now choose instead to buy the same capability from a respected health system that understands their business and unique data requirements.

Healthcare enterprises are also adopting innovation models that monetize data and clinical expertise to help promising digital health companies validate their solutions and potentially deploy them within the enterprise. Pittsburgh-based Highmark Health, one of the largest health plans in the country, has launched* a program that turns its internal innovation pro-gram VITAL into a commercial offering meant to help digital health start-ups test their products in real-world clinical envi-ronments. The core value of this program for start-ups is the access it provides to claims data on 4.5 million members that Highmark serves in three states. Mercy, based in St. Louis, Missouri, has launched† a real-world evidence network that will pool data from clinical networks across the country, start-ing with its database of clinical data from millions of patient records. Subscribers to the network, including researchers, regulators, and pharmaceutical and medical technology com-panies, will have access to this pool of deidentified data.

Many health systems have entered into data-sharing agree-ments with big tech firms with the near-term goal of using advanced analytics and machine-learning tools to gain insights on patients and drive improved healthcare outcomes. These partnerships between health systems and technology firms are becoming increasingly common. A 10-year partnership between Mayo Clinic and Google will allow Google Cloud to securely store the health system's data and work with Mayo clinicians to apply AI and machine learning to an array of complex use cases.‡ Industry associations such as the American Hospital Association and the Blue Cross Blue Shield Association have programs that provide opportunities for start-ups and innovators to tap into their member base for testing, validating, and commercializing innovation.

---

* Truong, Kevin. "Can Highmark Successfully Commercialize the Healthcare Innovation Process?" *MedCityNews*. April 14, 2019. Accessed December 13, 2019. https://medcitynews.com/2019/08/can-highmark-successfully-commercialize-the-healthcare-innovation-process/.

† Park, Andrea. "Mercy's IT Arm Launches Network for Clinical Data, Analytics." *Becker's Hospital Review*. August 14, 2019. Accessed December 13, 2019. www.beckershospitalreview.com/healthcare-information-technology/mercy-s-it-arm-launches-network-for-clinical-data-analytics.html.

‡ Miliard, Mike. "Mayo Clinic, Google Launch Major New 10-Year Partnership." *Healthcare IT News*. September 11, 2019. Accessed December 13, 2019. www.healthcareitnews.com/news/mayo-clinic-google-launch-major-new-10-year-partnership.

Many systems are looking to purchase rather than build such capabilities. If a health system already has a solid data platform, it could build a business. Additional revenue can be generated from selling or leasing deidentified data, and health systems can supplement their existing data with that from their willing data platform clients. One major health system we worked with is monetizing its innovation initiatives by exposing them as application programming interfaces (essentially, building blocks that facilitate software interoperability) to the external developer community.

Many leading health systems have been investing in AI and machine learning as an enabler of improved healthcare outcomes. The algorithms require significant time and effort to train and validate. If an organization has a library of algorithms that can potentially be used by a peer group health system, licensing them or entering into a mutually beneficial partnership to pool resources could improve overall outcomes in both organizations.

Payer Platform

With advances in digital, new capabilities in care management are emerging. Historically, providers have not done well when they added payer capabilities. Most went out of business and sold off their payer capabilities. Disruptive entrants like Oscar offer a payer product based on an all-digital platform. The payer platform has historically been manually intensive. With a digital platform, the barrier to entry is lowered. Providers may now have a second chance of entering the payer business. Leveraging tech as Oscar has, many of the previous manually intensive work can be displaced via automation. Engagement is enhanced with digital capabilities. While it has been challenging to be both a payer and provider, consider the success of Kaiser Permanente on the provider side. They are successful in part because of their reliance on digital capabilities. UnitedHealthcare has quietly amassed the largest physician panel, crossing over from the payer side. Powered by digital capabilities, the line between payer and provider is diminishing. Healthcare enterprises can now successfully be both or wait for a payer to displace them.

Brand Platform

Health systems have something that many tech companies do not have, and non-traditional players struggle for: brand loyalty. Most health systems have a robust brand within their communities. A few have a regional brand, and a select few, a national following. In all cases, the brand can be leveraged for additional impact and revenue. Health systems can leverage their brand with digital investments to generate additional revenue and in some cases develop customer stickiness, for example, with a telemedicine platform or hospitalist second opinion. Partnerships with a luxury retail brand could enable a virtual visit kiosk at every store. These opportunities are all enabled from digital investments. We discuss a few examples drawn from existing programs across the country today.

Health systems' franchise services could include spas, massage centers, and fitness facilities. In the competitive Texas market, Baylor Scott & White Health and Texas Health Resources both have opened several branded fitness centers. In fact, the Baylor Tom Landry Fitness Center even sponsors its own triathlon each year. Hackensack University Medical Center is largely credited with being the first major hospital to open its own spa. Banner Health and Memorial Hermann quickly followed suit. Fitness facilities, massage centers, and spas are a natural part of the wellness continuum and will generate additional income.* Other opportunities include branded clothing, co-branded IoT devices, and supplements. These services and

---

* American Spa Staff. *Hospital-Based Spas Offer Well-Rounded Approach to Healing.* March 4, 2006. Accessed January 29, 2020. www.americanspa.com/hospital-based-spas-offer-well-rounded-approach-healing.

products could be made available by leveraging new digital capabilities.

Large national retailers such as Walmart and Walgreens have created a market for retail care and taken customers away from traditional healthcare providers. Hospitals can preserve their market share and revenue by partnering and/ or expanding their services into retail settings. CVS has demonstrated that offering primary care and preventative services in a retail setting can help ensure a simple and smooth customer experience. The University of Pittsburgh Medical Center (UPMC) and CommonSpirit Health are two large hospital systems that have also begun to extend into retail initiatives, leading with a pharmacy.* Many leading systems, including Northwestern Memorial Hospital, Penn Hospital, NYU Langone Health, and Johns Hopkins Medicine, offer executive wellness and specific coaching programs.† To date we have not seen the return of investment analysis, but certainly the return on experience is high.

New businesses can be created by redeploying existing capabilities and enabling them with new technologies, an example of which is a life center. Life centers leverage multidisciplinary experts (e.g., dieticians and sports medicine clinicians) in one-stop virtual and physical places that focus on wellness and holistic medicine. With digital platforms in place, healthcare organizations can extend their reach by offering digital menus, nutrition counseling, and premade meals shipped to homes. These can be offered to athletes looking for healthy alternatives or busy households looking to source meal preparation. The most popular program at the Medical University of South Carolina is their weight

---

* Paavola, Alia. *6 Hospitals Investing in Retail, Specialty or In-House Pharmacy.* July 10, 2019. Accessed January 29, 2020. https://triblive.com/local/pittsburgh-al legheny/duquesne-university-pharmacy-on-centre-ave-sold-to-upmc/.

† Reeves, Benjamin. *10 Top Executive Wellness Programs.* October 7, 2014. Accessed January 29, 2020. www.worth.com/10-top-executive-well ness-programs/.

management program. The plan includes two sets of lab tests, individualized diet and exercise planning, eight weeks of meal replacements, fitness instruction, a pedometer, and weekly one-on-one meetings with registered dietitians, exercise physiologists, and psychologists.* Ohio State Medical Center and the University of Michigan Hospital have similar programs. A guiding principle should be: If you prescribe it, provide it.

Health monitoring services targeting everyone from athletes to the elderly can be digitally enabled using remote tracking and sensing devices. These capabilities extend health system services to the home, helping address cost and quality. UPMC and Einstein Healthcare Network provide health monitoring for their patients, and the trend is growing, with many other health systems following suit. UnitedHealthcare recently purchased health monitoring start-up Vivify,† whose investors include Ascension Health. Health monitoring capabilities are rapidly expanding and will become ubiquitous in the future. Coupled with artificial intelligence and machine learning, health monitoring services can alert patients before they fall or experience a host of other adverse events.

Telehealth Platform

In the emerging post COVID-19 era of digital health, many routine and urgent care services will be delivered through a virtual platform such as telehealth. Larger health systems can leverage investments in **telemedicine** and consider renting them in a platform-as-a-service model to other systems. An example of providing white-label services for others is the

---

* Campbell, Hannah. *15 Top Medical Weight Loss Centers.* January 8, 2014. Accessed January 29, 2020. www.health.com/weight-loss/15-top-medical-weight-loss-centers.
† Farr, Christina. *UnitedHealth, an Insurance Giant, Just Scooped Up Patient Monitoring Start-Up Vivify Health.* October 30, 2019. Accessed January 29, 2020. www.cnbc.com/2019/10/30/unitedhealthcare-acquires-vivify-health-patient-monitoring-start-up.html.

joint venture between American Well and Cleveland Clinic, called The Clinic. This new virtual health platform allows both companies to extend their brand and marketplace influence. EHR vendor Epic has created an extendable version of its EHR application known as Community Connect. Rather than buying its own expensive EHR, a hospital can rent the EHR of a partner health system. This program has proved immensely popular and generates additional revenue for the host organization while improving the patient experience.

In addition to the opportunities described above, there are more that health systems can consider exploring. One such opportunity area is cybersecurity. Healthcare providers are vigilant in protecting their patient data considering frequent cyberattacks and ransomware incidents. However, many providers do not have the internal capability to design and implement sophisticated cybersecurity programs and look to outside help. Health systems tend to trust other health systems more than a technology vendor. This creates an opportunity for sophisticated health systems with a strong cybersecurity platform to extend this as a service to others. Health systems that are further along in their digital transformation journey can also offer consulting services to help other systems accelerate digital transformation, especially in non-competing marketplaces. Consulting services require no new investments; by utilizing available hours in an associate's work schedule, health systems can convert these into billable hours for short-term engagements. In other words, digital transformation leaders can begin to recoup their investment by helping others in their respective journeys.

While many of the revenue monetization opportunities apply to larger health systems, smaller health systems can just as effectively utilize the same strategies by focusing on their strengths, such as their longitudinal patient data on local and regional populations, social determinants of health for their respective communities, and so on. They can also leverage scale economies for technology platform investments by partnering with other health systems, or even license their own IP and data assets to larger health systems, technology enterprises, or independent physician practices.

Innovation Platform

Some of the larger health systems have created their own innovation and venture divisions to generate additional revenue. In Table 2.1, we highlight the five largest innovation funds in healthcare today. The health systems are among the largest in the nation and the returns from their investments are increasingly contributing to the bottom line of the enterprise in meaningful ways. In 2018, Boston-based Partners HealthCare brought in $154 million in investment income from the commercialization of its innovation programs. Partners has a team of over 125 associates overseeing an investment portfolio that went from $35 million to $171 million in 10 years. Many health systems have long had internal functions to commercialize medical innovations. Digital health innovation offers

Table 2.1 Top venture innovation funds by health systems

Health system	Venture fund/ innovation	Fund details
Ascension Health	$800 million	Started in 1999, invested in more than 75 early-stage ventures
UPMC	$700 million	Invested in 80 different ventures in the last 20 years
Kaiser	$500 million	Invested in more than 65 companies over the last 20 years
Providence St. Joseph	$300 million	Invested in 15 companies since 2014
Partners HealthCare	$251 million	Invested in 37 portfolio companies and spin-offs

Source: Damo Consulting Research.

a new and potentially lucrative opportunity for additional revenue streams for health systems.

Health systems investing in innovation development can look to monetize the innovations by offering them as a service to other health systems. Often, these innovations may be developed on general-purpose technology platforms for specific use cases related to healthcare. One health system we have worked with has successfully licensed software developed on a third-party technology platform to other health systems.

Leading health systems are thoughtfully developing innovation models with a clear intention of generating significant incremental revenue opportunities. An example is a three-step approach at Providence Health. Whenever there is a need for a new capability, the innovation group at Providence looks at internal innovation for available solutions that can be leveraged, after which they proceed to scan the digital health marketplace for ready-to-deploy solutions. If neither approach yields results, they look at building the solution internally. New opportunities that have emerged from its innovation programs are carefully nurtured and incubated before being launched commercially as a stand-alone offering. This was the case with Xealth, a digital health platform developed in-house at Providence Health that has gone on to become an independent company in which several leading health systems have made strategic equity investments.

Key Takeaways and Action Steps

1. Healthcare organizations need to reimagine the primary care experience and enable consumers to access care online whenever they need it. Digital front doors are a powerful tool for differentiation and also the competitive landscape for control over the primary care experience of the future. Deep personalization and localization are becoming table stakes for healthcare providers.

2. Health systems should leverage the strong bonds between consumers and trusted physicians to deliver an integrated care delivery experience that emerging players cannot replicate. Health systems will need to go beyond EHR systems to prepare for a digital future. Health systems need to act with urgency to accelerate innovation to keep pace with digital transformation and the disruptive potential of well-funded, large, non-traditional players from the tech and non-tech worlds.

3. Health systems are competing on quality of care and the price at which it is delivered. They must explore partnerships with technology firms that bring advanced analytics capabilities to gain insights about their patient populations to improve their organizational performance. They must explore cost-saving opportunities through operational improvements in care delivery to enable investment in digital innovations.

4. Health systems can no longer rely solely on investment income and traditional reimbursement mechanisms. A by-product of digital transformation includes the ability to generate alternative forms of revenue related to brand, data, and consulting services.

5. Retreat idea: Gather a cross-functional team and brainstorm three to five alternative revenue opportunities for the enterprise.

THIRTY-SECOND AGILE CONSULT

What percentage of your patients accessed care through an online channel at the end of 2019? How many access it today, and what do you expect it to be in 12 months?

Chapter 3

Creating an Agile Digital Transformation Blueprint

The term "agile" is typically used in the context of software development to denote a nonlinear approach that relies on rapid iterations and a collaborative process through which solutions evolve gradually instead of being developed to a rigid set of specifications at the beginning of the process. We have adapted the definition of agile to outline a similar approach to developing a digital strategy and roadmap. Many blueprints or pathways for business processes are displayed in a process flow diagram or pyramid. They are often sequential. We challenge the notion that there is a strict linear process by which digital transformation occurs. Transformation of any kind begins with action. Do not let perfect be the enemy of good. Leveraging an agile methodology, health systems can move forward nonlinearly. The recent pandemic showcased the power of agility in responding to crisis. Refined, this is the new way of work for digitally transformative organizations. We focus on three stages for building a digital transformation blueprint:

1. Develop a digital strategy and assess the organization's readiness for transformation.

2. Build a digital transformation roadmap and prioritize the initiatives.
3. Follow an agile digital transformation model and select your digital platform partners.

A Vision for a Digital Enterprise

One of the first issues that healthcare executives and the technology firms that serve them need to address is what digital transformation means for their enterprise. If healthcare organizations are unable to articulate their vision, they will never find their way. As part of the research for this book, we decided to find out how leading organizations define digital transformation. Table 3.1 is a sample of formal definitions of digital transformation that we found.

The definitions in Table 3.1 highlight the wide variations in the definitions of digital transformation and the challenges of defining it in simple terms. There is simply no universal definition. This is further evidence of why it is critical that organizations create or adopt a definition that best represents their transformation objectives. The variations are also indicative of the perspective of the individual organizations that may be defining digital transformation to suit their own business goals and needs. As we see it, digital transformation is a reimagining of the business through a combination of technology, data, people, and processes.

We did not find a formal definition of digital or digital transformation in any major health system's website. We frequently came across quotes such as this, from Intermountain Healthcare's CEO Marc Harrison:

> Our aspiration is to be the first digitally enabled, consumer-centric integrated delivery system in the U.S. We are taking cues from Amazon, fintechs, Starbucks, and the like. We are going to inject that holistically into a real

digital transformation of an integrated health system to truly understand and serve people the way they want to be served.*

Table 3.1 Digital transformation definitions

Organization	Definition of digital transformation
Salesforce	Digital transformation is the process of using digital technologies to create new – or modify existing – business processes, culture, and customer experiences to meet changing business and market requirements. This reimagining of business in the digital age is digital transformation[†]
Microsoft	Digital transformation is about reimagining how you bring together people, data, and processes. A digital transformation strategy that focuses on these three pillars will help you to create value for your customers and maintain a competitive advantage in a digital-first world[‡]
Gartner	Digital business transformation is the process of exploiting digital technologies and supporting capabilities to create a robust new digital business model[§]

(Continued)

handwritten annotations: impact, CX, 3 elements, Service to Veterans, Goal #1 Logos definition, Cross-functional alignment

---

* Intermountain Healthcare. *What the World Is Saying About Us.* 2019 November. Accessed December 13, 2019. https://intermountainhealthcare.org/about/who-we-are/trustee-resource-center/newsletter/newsletter-archive/intermountain-in-the-news--november-2017/.

† "What Is Digital Transformation?" Salesforce. Accessed December 13, 2019.

‡ "What Is Digital Transformation?" Microsoft. Accessed December 13, 2019. https://www.microsoft.com/en-mt/digitaltransformation/.

§ "Gartner Glossary." Gartner. Accessed December 13, 2019. https://www.gartner.com/en/information-technology/glossary/digital-business-transformation.

handwritten annotations: holistic support, Common language, Common Voice

Table 3.1 (Continued)   Digital transformation definitions

Organization	Definition of digital transformation
Forrester	Digital transformation is not just about technology; it is about reimagining your company. It is the necessary but challenging journey of operating digital-first with the speed and nimbleness to change or introduce new products and experiences rapidly, exploit technology to create lean operations, and free people to do more complex tasks that create value[§]
Bain & Company	Digital transformations integrate digital technologies into an organization's strategy and operations. Focusing the entire organization on opportunities to merge the best of both digital and physical worlds, digital transformations examine each link in the customer experience chain, explore new technology links that can bolster the base business, and weave them into holistic systems that create superior customer experiences. The process aims to profoundly extend competitive advantages and accelerate profitable growth[*]
BCG	Digital transformation: in business, a fundamental change, a metamorphosis, in how companies generate value for their owners and other stakeholders, achieved by applying digital technologies and ways of working to all aspects of the business[†]

Source: Company websites.

[§] "Differentiate with Digital." Forrester. Accessed December 13, 2019. https://go.forrester.com/digital-transformation/.

[*] Bain & Company. 2018. *Management Tools Digital Transformation.* April 8. Accessed December 13, 2019. https://www.bain.com/insights/management-tools-digital-transformation/.

[†] "Digital Transformation." BCG. Accessed December 13, 2019. https://www.bcg.com/digital-bcg/digital-transformation/overview.aspx.

The leaders we worked with understand that digital transformation needs sponsorship at the highest levels of the organization. They also appreciate that digital transformation is not an information technology initiative per se. It is more about organizational and cultural change supported by new and innovative digital technologies. This raises questions around who should be involved in developing and driving digital transformation.

The answers vary from enterprise to enterprise; however, one thing on which everyone agrees is the need to involve stakeholders across the enterprise. In one case, to ensure that digital did not become yet another IT initiative, the CIO invited an extended group of leaders from across the enterprise to be a part of the digital innovation roadmap development process. The response was overwhelming. The CIO eventually decided to create two groups. The first one comprised cross-functional representatives from various divisions, including clinical departments to provide guidance and oversight to the process. A smaller group of a dozen or so hand-selected individuals would be the core team involved in developing the roadmap. This included a mix of formal and informal leaders and a patient. The CIO realized that it is critical to include not only formally identified leaders but also key organizational influencers.

The digital transformation journey begins with developing a vision for the enterprise. With a vision and definition in place, an assessment of the current maturity level and enterprise readiness for digital transformation is critical. This starts with fundamental questions about digital aspirations for the enterprise. The maturity model described in detail in Figure 1.2 in Chapter 1 is a good starting point for health systems to evaluate their current state. It is also important to remember that digital transformation is a journey, not a destination. The value of technology in improving care quality is often intangible, and it is even more so when investing in an uncertain digital future. While being good stewards for the organization's resources, healthcare leaders also must avoid succumbing to short-termism in considering digital transformation invest-ments. Digital transformation is a culture, not a project.

Figure 3.1 shows at a high level the four pillars of an enter-prise-level digital strategy.

Engaging patients and enabling caregivers directly relate to how care will be delivered in the future. Driving operational efficiencies is how the administrative functions of a healthcare enterprise – human resources, legal, supply chain, finance – can be improved through digital initiatives. The fourth area, enriching community, is missional and part of every organi-zation's community benefit mandate. How do health systems improve the health of the populations around them? Some of the highest rates of infant mortality and poverty exist in the neighborhoods surrounding some of the most prestigious organizations.

There is one more aspect to digital transformation: creating new lines of revenue. As reimbursement models change and reimbursement shrinks, health systems must create new reve-nue models if they are to stay solvent. We have discussed new revenue opportunities briefly in Chapter 2.

While there is an increased focus on addressing burnout and bringing joy back to the practice of medicine as reflected in the expanded quadruple aim of healthcare* (the original triple aim being reducing costs of care, improving quality of outcomes, and improving patient experience), a lot of focus has also been on programs that improve patient experiences. Digital health solutions that virtualize care delivery, such as

Figure 3.1   Key focus areas for healthcare's digital transformation

* Feeley, Derek. *The Triple Aim or the Quadruple Aim? Four Points to Help Set Your Strategy*. November 28, 2017. Accessed January 29, 2020. http://www.ihi.org/c ommunities/blogs/the-triple-aim-or-the-quadruple-aim-four-points-to-help-set-your-strategy.

telehealth and remote monitoring, are strategic bets for health systems today.

We recommend an approach to digital transformation that is holistic and enterprise-wide, addressing the four pillars described in Figure 3.1. Here are some considerations while launching enterprise-level digital transformation initiatives:

- Digital transformation often begins as a departmental initiative in large multi-hospital systems. While this is an excellent approach to experiment with innovation, a significant barrier to increased adoption is the lack of resources and executive-level sponsorship for enterprise-level deployment. This can lead to suboptimal use of the technology and a failure to tap into learnings from across the enterprise.
- The technology solution landscape for enterprise-level digital platforms is not mature, and no single platform can meet all the digitalization needs of healthcare enterprises. This requires a best-of-breed approach that creates governance and technology integration challenges. One of the significant challenges with this approach is ensuring that systems integrate and interoperate with each other to support digital transformation.
- Technical debt accumulated over the years can divert scarce resources from innovation and digital transformation toward addressing infrastructure shortcomings and application upgrades.
- Despite the high activity levels in the digital health start-up space, the number of viable and proven last-mile solutions for developing engaging and efficient patient and caregiver experiences is relatively limited. Many digital health start-ups lack resources as well as a critical mass of live customer deployments, which increases the risks for healthcare enterprises considering deploying solutions by start-ups. Many leading health systems have developed governance models to evaluate start-ups, guide them

through enterprise-wide adoption, and manage technology and financial risks.

- Digital health solutions need significant customization and often lack robust integration with EHR and other systems. It becomes incumbent on the healthcare enterprise to invest in configuring the solutions for the enterprise's needs and building an infrastructure to integrate with systems of record.
- Many digital health programs lack a reimbursement model, which makes it harder to justify the investments. In such cases, the returns often must be computed in terms of strategic and intangible benefits with a long-term view.

Digital transformation is primarily a cross-functional business initiative that requires a tremendous culture change. In our work with leading health systems, the world's biggest technology solution providers, and innovative start-ups, we've seen that the singular challenge has been to go beyond paying lip service to digital and to lay out a digital roadmap that can be executed with ready-to-deploy technologies.

Developing a digital strategy and a detailed roadmap for digital transformation enables leaders to articulate an enterprise-wide view of what the transformation looks like, how long it will take, and how much it will cost (Figure 3.2). In this section, we will cover the three phases of a digital transformation journey at a high level and discuss critical aspects of the journey.

Digital Strategy and Readiness Assessment

Digital Strategy and Enterprise Vision

- Where does digital transformation fit in overall enterprise strategy?

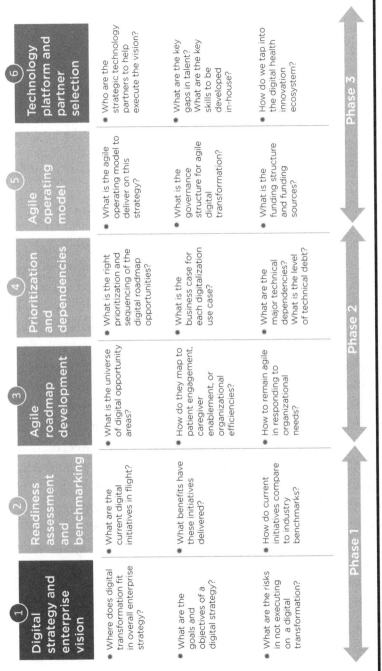

Figure 3.2   A phased approach to digital transformation. Source: Damo Consulting Inc.

- What are the goals and objectives of a digital strategy?
- How will you measure these and who is responsible?
- What are the risks in not executing on a digital transformation?

Readiness Assessment and Benchmarking

- What are the current digital initiatives in flight?
- What benefits have these initiatives delivered?
- How do current initiatives compare to industry benchmarks?

Digital transformation strategy should follow a clear set of enterprise goals around digitally enabling the organization for the future. At Cleveland Clinic, for example, the pre-pandemic enterprise goals included shifting 50 percent of outpatient visits to virtual visits and 25 percent of in-patient days to at-home stays, providing clear guidance for prioritizing initiatives in a digital transformation roadmap.* Digital transformation leaders should also evaluate the current state of their digital transformation against those of peers in the industry. One health system we worked with conducted extensive research on published information about digital innovation programs across leading health systems across the country; launched an internal survey to gather input and views on what digital means internally to leaders across functions; and reached out to peer organizations, leading technology and consulting firms, and industry analysts to learn their views on what digital means to them and to the clients they serve. The detailed information gathered from this exercise helped assess the digital maturity of the organization and informed the setting of priorities in implementing individual initiatives in a digital transformation roadmap.

Enterprise readiness is a critical factor to assess before launching a digital transformation program. Readiness

---

* Rasmussen, Peter and Paddy Padmanabhan. "Developing a Digital Health Roadmap – The Cleveland Clinic Experience." Filmed September 2019 at Society for Healthcare Strategy & Market Development Connections, Nashville, TN. *Video*, 57:36. https://www.youtube.com/watch?v=95_5KqDMIjg.

assessments require evaluating organizational appetite for digital transformation, a clear understanding of the gaps and opportunities in patient and caregiver experiences, the maturity level of enterprise IT capabilities, and investments in upgrading IT infrastructure. A significant factor in IT readiness is technical debt, which refers to the level of investment required to upgrade the IT infrastructure to be ready to meet the digital aspirations of the enterprise. Other factors include free cash flow for investments, capacity for large-scale change management, and a stable and reliable technology partner ecosystem.

A self-assessment of readiness levels can start by looking at current in-flight initiatives and their maturity levels. The list of questions in Table 3.2 will help identify resources, challenges, roadblocks, and best practices to establish a baseline and

Table 3.2 Sample questions for an internal survey on digital initiatives

1. Name and describe the digital initiatives currently deployed in the enterprise.
2. What have been the achievements of such efforts to date?
3. How do you measure success (key metrics)?
4. What investment has gone into these programs so far (last one to two years)?
5. Do you have a view of the future state for your initiative?
6. What kinds of resources do you need to get to that future state?
7. Is there a documented business plan/case for investment? If not, how do you plan to fund your initiative?
8. How does your initiative enable new care models or change existing care models?
9. What challenges do you foresee in the development and adoption of your initiative?
10. Who are your "first adopters?" How will their experience and results be leveraged to accelerate adoption by other users?
11. What are the risks associated with your program and how do you plan to mitigate them?
12. What internal/external technology capabilities are required to enable the transformation (or to implement your initiative)?

Source: Damo Consulting Inc.

determine a strategy going forward. We recommend administering these questions via an online survey tool and inviting responses from across functions and departments to obtain as comprehensive a view as possible.

The internal survey should include a series of questions around how digital transformation could positively impact the work of caregivers, how to implement the transformation, and what kinds of tools and technologies would be required. An important question is whether the enterprise has the internal capability to handle the scale and scope of the transformation and what kind of partners the enterprise would need for the journey.

Based on an internal survey we conducted at a health system along the lines described above, we were able to identify key stakeholder needs and align them to the digital transformation goals of the enterprise (Table 3.3). We were able to categorize the responses into specific transformational aspects and align them to stakeholder needs. The exercise gave us valuable insights into where the enterprise should focus its priorities as it relates to the stakeholder groups they serve.

A thoughtful mapping of transformation aspects to the individual journeys of patients and caregivers, such as the one in Table 3.3, is necessary to ensure alignment among stakeholder groups. As an example, improving communication is important for improving patient access as well as caregiver collaboration. Reducing friction in scheduling appointments is an important need for patients, and enabling remote monitoring was a key requirement for caregivers to improve the quality of care and outcomes.

The decision to invest in a digital initiative may not just be tied to the needs of a specific stakeholder group, but also address other systemic issues. Consider the case of Geisinger Health System below.

John Kravitz, CIO, Geisinger Health System states that a big priority for his organization is improving access to care. One of the use case scenarios that he and his team have focused on for their digital strategy is scheduling patient appointments and the potential to use emerging technologies such

Table 3.3 Aligning digital enablers to improvement areas

Stakeholder	Digital enabler	Improvement area
Patients	Communication: easier communication between patients and caregivers; tools to help patients maintain their care plans and wellness while they are at home	Engagement
	Process: simplification of procedures to reduce friction for patients in finding a scheduled appointment	Access
	Care models: new care models for patients in their homes with ongoing medical support through digital interactions	Care delivery
Caregivers	Remote monitoring: enable physicians to engage patients remotely and to train and engage other physicians remotely	Engagement
	Communication: easier communication between caregivers	Collaboration
	Virtualization: tools that allow physicians to practice care when not co-located with physicians or patients	Care delivery

Source: Damo Consulting Inc.

as chatbots or digital assistants to enhance the processes beyond their contact centers. There is another dynamic at play as well. Geisinger Health System employs around 2,300 associates for contact center operations that enable patients to manage appointments, and it is an area with significant attrition. Because of its criticality to their business, Kravitz and his leadership team look at patient access as one of the first points for digital strategy to really focus on: fulfilling the need of outward-facing work with customers. Kravitz and his team are also exploring technologies such as biometric identification to improve the patient registration experience, adding convenient payment options at the time of registration, and wayfinding apps to help patients navigate their way around campus.

In the survey example we describe above, survey respondents saw opportunities for digitalization in healthcare mainly around telemedicine and virtual care. However, there were several essential use cases related to organizational efficiencies and community engagement that emerged during our subsequent discussions. Over time, survey responses were fleshed out to identify over 150 digital transformation opportunities, which were mapped to detailed journey maps for each category of stakeholders. We describe journey maps in greater detail in the next section.

The final step in readiness assessment is the benchmarking process to understand how the organization stacks up against peer group health systems. We recommend conducting site visits with peer group health systems, talking to strategic technology partners, and taking advantage of published research by analyst firms. When we conducted the benchmarking process for a large health system, we found a wide range of definitions of digital transformation and a relatively narrow range of digital initiatives that focused primarily on patient access and engagement through telehealth and digital marketing programs. For many, their EHR vendor had also become their digital platform of choice.

The Healthcare Information Management and Systems Society (HIMSS) has developed an online digital self-assessment tool that can be useful. The Digital Health Indicator measures progress toward a digital health ecosystem. An ecosystem that connects clinicians and provider teams with people, enabling them to manage their health and wellness using digital tools in a secure and private environment whenever and wherever care is needed. Operational and care delivery processes are outcomes-driven, informed by data and real-world evidence to achieve exceptional quality, safety and performance that is sustainable.

When we spoke with technology solution providers, we discovered, not surprisingly, that each firm had a definition of digital transformation that aligned with whatever they had to sell; the most common technology themes equated digital with cloud, advanced analytics, or automation. We learned more about the limitations of these definitions when we dug deeper into developing a roadmap and prioritizing digital initiatives as part of our own work. When we spoke with analyst firms, we gained valuable insights from their work with other sectors that are further ahead in their digital transformation journeys, such as the banking and hospitality industries. These insights ignited fresh thinking around the challenges of healthcare and what is possible when developing digital strategies.

Agile Roadmap Development and Prioritization of Initiatives

Digital Roadmap Development

- What does the landscape of digital opportunities look like?
- How do they map to patient engagement, caregiver enablement, organizational efficiencies, or community enrichment?
- How to remain agile in adjusting to organizational needs?

Prioritization and Dependencies

- What is the right prioritization and sequencing of initiatives in the digital transformation roadmap?
- What is the business case for each digital initiative?
- How to ensure agility in executing the initiatives?

Developing a digital transformation roadmap requires a detailed understanding of the experience of the stakeholders involved: patients, caregivers, and administrators. Journey maps are a useful tool for understanding enterprise-level digital needs. A patient journey map, for instance, is a way to understand the patient experience through a detailed sequence of the various touchpoints with their healthcare provider. At one health system, we used journey mapping to identify the digital opportunities at every stage of a stakeholder journey. We then mapped them to the required technology investments and IT infrastructure dependencies. Based on our experience across health systems, here is a sample of what a high-level journey map looks like for a typical integrated health system.

The patient journey map and the digitalization opportunities in each phase were then combined with the enabling and foundational technologies involved (Table 3.4). The patient journey is broken into four stages: activate, engage, care, and nurture. Within each stage, there could be several substages. For illustrative purposes, we divided the care phase into outpatient, in-patient, post-acute, and at-home care.

The dependency between digital technologies and the enabling IT infrastructure is an important consideration in implementing digital initiatives. Many digital initiatives often fail or are suboptimal in their impact due to the lack of a strong underlying technology foundation. As an example, a robust wireless network is necessary for seamless communication between caregivers using smart wireless-enabled devices. For cloud-enabled technologies that interface with on-premises systems, the network architecture must be designed to minimize latency issues for mission-critical patient applications.

Journey maps are an important tool in developing digital health solutions for individual use cases. Many digital health innovators and start-ups use journey maps as a core tool in their approach to designing solutions. Healthcare enterprises are now recognizing that designing intuitive, engaging, and seamless digital experiences is critical not only to better engaging patients in their healthcare, but also for improving convenience and dealing with the emerging competitive

Table 3.4 Patient experience journeys and technology components

Journey phase		Required capability	Enabling technology	Foundational technology
Activate		• Individualized campaigns, social listening • Linkages to lifestyle (e.g. listening) • Online/centralized scheduling • Provider directory/access • Costs /out-of-pocket estimation /pre-auth	• CRM • Marketing automation • Social media • Financial calculators	• Networks • Data center • Unified communications • Compute devices • Cloud • ERP • EHR • Data warehouse/ data lakes • AI/machine learning (ML)
Engage		• Virtual check-in, geotracking • Bi-directional 1-1 text (e.g, for appointment updates) • Transportation support, valet service • Real-time, multiparty, synchronous communication	• Telemedicine platforms • Beacons • Secure messaging • Kiosks	
Care	Outpatient In-patient Post-acute	• Triage for directing patients to the right caregiver/right • Place/right time/intensity of service • Remote monitoring	• Voice recognition • IoT recognition • Data visualization • AR/VR • Intelligent hospital rooms • Remote monitoring • Pop health tools • Gamification	
	Home	• Enabling patient involvement/inputs to the visit documentation • Digital platform for engaging families and others in the patient's care (episodic and chronic) • Pop health/chronic condition management • Automated prescription refills		
Nurture		• Automated prescription refills • Automated feedback • Billing, financial/payment options • Referral management	• Intelligent automation • Chronic care management platforms • Alerts and notifications	

Source: Damo Consulting Inc.

landscape. Inspired by the highly intuitive user experiences in consumer-facing applications, healthcare as a sector has been catching up with the importance of design in digital health experiences. Human-centered design is a new discipline that is driving patient experience and patient engagement. When we talk about human-centered design in the context of healthcare consumers, we do not think of just the provider and the patient, but all of the people who are part of the healthcare relationship. Human-centered design is the process of designing and building any product or service, starting with an understanding of user needs. This understanding of user needs then defines the use cases, requirements, and principles that drive all subsequent decisions, from the architecture to the form factor, ergonomics, and interface components.

Design is the primary competitive advantage being leveraged by giants of the tech world. One of the common threads that define success for Apple, Uber, Facebook, Google, and others is design. While most healthcare organizations are adept in continuous process improvement, design thinking requires a new skill set and approach.

Human-centered design is about more than just a superior interface. Digital front doors, adequately wrapped around core EHR systems, can deliver significantly better user experiences, at least at the interface level. However, human-centered design in healthcare is a multidisciplinary practice that includes agile software development, lean methodologies, data interoperability, privacy and security, and a host of other factors. By combining design effectively with tech, organizations can increase engagement, improve outcomes, reduce costs, and bring joy back to medicine – in other words, meet the quadruple aim of healthcare.

Journey maps and human-centered design are increasingly now part of the toolkit for digital transformation leaders, enabling them to not just identify what solutions need to be implemented as part of a digital roadmap, but also how to build them in a way that meets the enhanced expectations of consumers today.

Once the use cases have been identified and defined, the next step is to prioritize them in a digital transformation roadmap. Digital transformation is mostly about cultural and organizational change. However, even with high levels of organizational readiness and support, it is not possible for any large-scale transformation program to be implemented all at once. The prioritization matrix shown in Figure 3.3 highlights the need to show near-term wins, mainly as a confidence-building exercise for the C-suite and the board of directors. It establishes credibility for the digital innovation team and strengthens their hand when seeking additional investments. Near-term wins in the form of new initiatives with short pay-back periods are understandably popular with the C-suite, but also deliver immediate benefits to patients or caregivers. An example of this is a simple virtual check-in application in a pediatric care facility that includes a wait-time estimator and ensures that the patients and their parents do not lose their

Figure 3.3 Digital innovation prioritization matrix. Source: Damo Consulting Inc.

place in line if they are running late. Another is a "know-me" feature that allows staff at the patient registration desk to greet individuals by name and pull up basic profile information that reduces the time taken registering patients.

Feature enhancements can often deliver a moderate amount of impact with not much effort, an example of which is the use of voice recognition to read patient medical information from EHR systems, which can improve caregiver efficiency and the quality of the patient experience by allowing the doctor to have more face time with the patient.

Game-changers and long-term bets are typically complex initiatives that require a high upfront investment (e.g., a customer relationship management system) or have a long and uncertain payback, such as cloud enabling a data and analytics infrastructure at the enterprise level.

A prioritization matrix is a useful tool for yet another reason: It is almost impossible to implement all the required digital initiatives in a roadmap at once, especially if the wish list includes a hundred applications or more. Once the prioritization matrix is filled out, it should be quickly mapped to the inventory of digital innovation currently in progress within the health system. Most health systems have some form of a digital innovation program underway in siloed departmental initiatives, which can be evaluated for enterprise-level rollout. Often, EHR systems and other existing technologies in the enterprise IT stack include many capabilities that may meet the near-term needs of a digital experience platform, an example of which would be a scheduling and messaging application available in the EHR system. Other native capabilities such as data analytics, system integration, and mobile application development can also be leveraged across the enterprise.

The prioritization matrix is a useful guide to communicate with stakeholders involved in the implementation of a digital roadmap. In addition to providing clarity on digitalization priorities, it is helpful as a tool for planning and budgeting for the necessary investments. The prioritization matrix also serves as a useful portfolio management tool, helping the enterprise understand the scale and scope of the initiatives, investment allocations, risk levels, and payback periods.

Aaron Martin, Chief Digital Officer at Providence Health, prioritizes the many problems and opportunities into what he refers to as "needle movers." Sara Vaezy, the head of Digital Strategy at Providence Health and part of Martin's team, leads an internal consulting group and works with clinical and operations leaders from across the 116,000-person organization to identify and then scope, size, and prioritize these needle movers. The exercise is repeated every three years and then incrementally every single year. By following this approach, Martin, Vaezy, and their team have identified over a hundred problems from these discussions, boiled them down to the top 35, and put a value on each of them. The value could be economic value, clinical value, or in terms of the mission of the organization. Once they have assigned a value, they engage the organization around how to solve individual problems using a digital approach and an innovation model.

Agile Digital Transformation and Technology Partner Selection

Agile Digital Transformation Model

- How is agile different from the conventional approach to transformation?
- What is the optimal operating structure to deliver on a digital strategy?
- What is the governance structure for digital transformation?
- What are the funding guidelines and funding sources?

Technology Platform and Partner Selection

- What are the key gaps in talent? What are the key skills to be developed in-house?
- Who are the strategic technology partners to help execute the vision?
- How do we tap into the digital health start-up ecosystem?

Digital transformation is often slow because of the burden of traditional organizational processes as they relate to technology. In traditional models, organizations complete each component in sequence. This is referred to as a waterfall approach (Figure 3.4). You complete one set of tasks or building blocks before completing the next. The paradigm is intuitive but not always relevant in this era.

In one health system, we wanted to demonstrate our prowess for developing a digital front door in a matter of weeks, not months. Using agile methods with corresponding two-week "sprints," we unveiled our minimally viable product in 12 weeks. While we were perfecting our culture and investing in infrastructure, we were constantly moving forward in our digital transformation. We continued to leverage our digital transformation teams and the patients who provided critical guidance. While we worked on modernizing our data analytics, we also finalized a critical joint venture that allowed us to vastly expand our virtual medicine capabilities.

An agile digital transformation model is visualized in Figure 3.4. The agile digital transformation model has six distinct subcomponents – culture, infrastructure, apps, data, design, and experience. We have described the subcomponents in detail in various chapters. These are the same required components for traditional digital transformation, but in our model the work of digital transformation can begin at any point in the process.

Born out of software development, agile has reinvented the way small and large projects are managed. In many cases, adopting agile methodologies saves time, reduces costs, and

Traditional Digital Transformation Climb

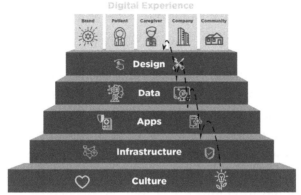

Agile Digital Transformation Flow

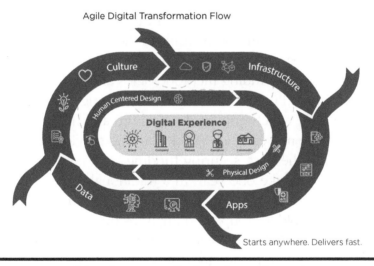

Figure 3.4   Traditional versus agile digital transformation

increases customer satisfaction. When undergoing digital transformation, it may be tempting to execute a traditional waterfall approach. It is certainly possible to undertake digital transformation with this approach, but it may unnecessarily prolong the process.

Most organizations admit that their infrastructure is far from digital ready. Legacy data centers and duplicate applications contribute to organizations' technical debt. Significant resources would be required to fully prepare existing infrastructure for digital transformation. We suggest that any digital initiative taking more than two years is already outdated and out of touch.

Health systems should leverage agile in two ways. The first is to use agile process and methodologies in software application development, which we describe in Chapter 4. The second is to use agile principles in driving digital transformation initiatives at an enterprise level. With an agile approach to digital transformation, organizations can start anywhere in the model shown in Figure 3.4. It may be necessary to work through multiple iterations to address individual components, but completing one step before another in a linear fashion is no longer a requirement. Just start. In the digital age, time is the most precious commodity. Agile is the currency.

One of the barriers to digital transformation is an insistence on using outdated funding methodologies and processes. Most health systems still approach funding in the digital era as they did in the past, which only leads to failure and frustration. The digital age moves much faster than the previous business generation. In the past, securing funding for a new product or service could take one year. In a traditional funding model, digital transformation leaders are likely to have to go through multiple stakeholder groups and analyses before reaching decision-makers. With a sole focus on traditional return on investment, some transformation services and products that are focused on return on experience will never be approved and funded. Instead, we recommend adopting a new way to vet opportunities that enables digital transformation.

In a traditional model, it can take two to three years and most of the available capital to build culture and infrastructure before realizing any digital transformation benefits. In today's rapidly evolving technology and marketplace, that is an entire "digital generation". Digital is not a big project with a start and finish (traditional). It is a journey and should be planned and executed as such (agile). A sequential approach will no longer suffice. Applying agile methods and processes is now a competitive differentiator.

We recommend benchmarking your organization against your peer group health systems in terms of size and nature of the populations served and setting aside a budget that reflects the investment needs for digital transformation initiatives required to compete in the marketplace. Set up a governing body that is responsible for ensuring that technology investments are reviewed periodically and also has the authority to make changes to funding priorities as required in an agile fashion. With this approach, investment priorities can be continually reappraised and approval cycles for new investments can be significantly reduced. As a thumb rule, it should take no more than three months from when an idea is hatched to when it is funded using an agile governance model.

Strategic partnerships can also provide an additional funding source. The partnership approach we discuss in the next section as well as in Chapters 6 and 7 should include investments made by the partner company as well as by co-investments. Many vendors will gladly co-invest in a new technology platform or feature in return for the opportunity to gain validation and earn a reference site for future sales of the product.

EHR vendors have contributed a great deal to the safer practice of medicine. Digital transformation is predicated upon a strong clinical foundation that must include a robust EHR. A strong partnership between the health system and its EHR vendor is the key, particularly when the health system has a voice in future enhancements and direction. However, digital transformation should go beyond simply optimizing the EHR. It will be difficult – if not impossible – for health systems to undergo a digital transformation if they are primarily dependent on their vendor.

EHR vendors have many hurdles to jump that reduce their ability to respond quickly enough to the market. First, healthcare is a heavily regulated industry. It takes an inordinate amount of effort for vendors to develop software and ensure it complies with the myriad of rules and regulations. Second, the healthcare industry is complex, and the nature of the work (life and death) has made it a risk-averse culture. Finally, health organizations themselves are slow to make decisions and change. The entire ecosystem inadvertently slows progress. Often, organizations can transform more quickly by working with vendors who are small and nimble, complementing and enhancing what EHR vendors do rather than replicating it.

We recommend that health systems work closely with their EHR vendors in all transformation initiatives. As the team develops strategies, roadmaps, and platforms, digital transformation leaders should include their vendors in those discussions. While including their sales and account teams, it is also important to speak directly with the vendor's research and development teams and senior leaders. The vendor can bring experiences from other clients that will help health systems on their digital transformation journey. As the strategy matures and a roadmap is developed, the team should ask to see the vendor's one- to three-year roadmaps. Exploit synergies where they are available. There is no reason to develop a duplicative capability. The vendors may be able to adjust and accelerate their timelines to match that of the health system. Perhaps they can develop together. If it becomes clear that the vendor will not have the necessary capabilities in the next one to two years, the health system can develop that capability or find another partner to help. Health systems should not put their digital transformation solely in the hands of an EHR vendor.

We have found that EHR vendors are interested in engaging with organizations on their journey. This level of engagement is important for an organization to make wise decisions. It is important for both the industry and the patients that the EHR vendor hears the voice of the customer.

Once the collaboration with the EHR vendor and the digital transformation roadmap is in place, the big challenge is how to execute a large-scale digital transformation program with agility and speed. In this section, we discuss our experience in identifying program components and building a digital platform architecture. A typical digital platform architecture will have several components and will include a variety of platforms, unique to individual health systems. It is important to remember that there is no single vendor platform that includes all the components of an ideal digital platform. While EHR systems are foundational for clinical workflow management, organizations must look at emerging technology choices and seek out new strategic partners to execute the digital vision. We describe vendor categories through the ICEA™ framework in Chapter 6 and vendor stratification models in Chapter 7. Regardless of your vendor choices, agility, urgency, and speed are essential for implementing an enterprise-level digital roadmap.

We deliberately refer to "designing and building" a digital architecture because there is no single end-to-end platform in the marketplace that can substantially meet the needs of a comprehensive enterprise-level digital transformation roadmap. Health system leaders must build their digital architecture using a combination of existing technology investments, new strategic partnerships, and innovation management.

Digital transformation requires an ecosystem of strategic partnerships. By conducting thorough research on the technology solution marketplace, digital transformation leaders can identify the potential candidates that could meet the enterprise's needs for implementing the required digital architecture. Engaging an outside consulting firm at this stage could be valuable in identifying and evaluating the different platform options, the reputation and maturity of different digital solution providers, and the culture fit with the enterprise. The assessment of potential partners needs to be simple in the initial stages. Evaluate the firm's product features and conduct reference checks with the solution provider's customers to assess the maturity and stability of the product. Assess the level of effort required to implement the partner's platform and whether it is necessary to budget for additional costs for professional services. Evaluate the solution provider's implementation partner ecosystem; many technology companies have small or nonexistent professional services arms and will leave it to clients to select an implementation partner. Seek to implement the solution in a phased manner to manage risks, especially if the solution provider or platform is relatively new in the market.

No single solution provider today can address all the needs of a digital transformation program, despite technology vendor claims to the contrary. However, researching potential partners could determine if any of them could be a lead provider and take on the role of ecosystem integrator to manage multiple smaller providers. Often, a large systems integrator firm takes on this role for its clients and works with multiple technology partners to enable smooth implementation.

Many big technology firms with vast financial resources have committed themselves to making a big impact on healthcare. Several have launched "health cloud" platforms that are positioned as enterprise-level digital experience platforms that connect with foundational EHR systems for data and provide advanced analytics capabilities as well as rich development environments to encourage the start-up community to build innovative solutions. While tech firms' breadth and depth of capabilities are critical, culture remains the elusive yet key success criterion. Culture may include several attributes such as price transparency (simple and easy to understand without hidden items in small print), ease of contracting and flexibility with terms (watch out for resistance to business associate agreements), responsiveness and follow-through on commitments, and an organization-wide ethos of commitment to customer success. If health systems select a vendor based only on a list of technical capabilities, they are not likely to succeed.

We go into a detailed assessment of the technology provider landscape in Chapter 6.

Digital transformation often requires mining the existing digital health innovation ecosystem, especially start-ups, for end-user applications and point solutions that will enhance the consumer experience. Many start-ups focus on solving a specific problem in healthcare delivery, and they are often the only ones in that class. Larger health systems also have in-house innovation groups that develop these "last-mile" or point solutions. The big technology firms, for their part, have chosen not to invest in building last-mile solutions.* As an example, providers of customer relationship management solutions offer a platform on which developers and innovators can build point solutions or applications for specific consumer needs for specific industries. Health systems need to recognize that there is an implied commitment to a vendor platform for the long term, which requires a careful evaluation of platform choices when selecting the partner.

One question we are often asked relates to the proliferation of digital health start-ups. Innovation groups in healthcare organizations are often charged with identifying and deploying promising solutions from start-ups. However, there are several risks associated with deploying the solutions in a hospital environment, not least of which is the likelihood of patient harm. "We're seeing an explosion of digital health apps. Does anyone really know how well they work?" asks John Halamka, who is leading digital innovation for the Mayo Clinic as President of the Mayo Clinic Platform. Digital health innovation is at a crossroads today. There has never been a greater need for the innovation that digital health start-ups bring to healthcare. At the same time, the funding, contracting, and commercialization of innovation from these start-ups are constrained

---

* Padmanabhan, Paddy. "Digital Health's Last Mile Problem." CIO. May 18, 2018. Accessed December 13, 2019. https://www.cio.com/article/3274446/digital-health-s-last-mile-problem.html.

by the lack of appetite for risk, the lack of a reimbursement model, and the administrative overhead involved in managing multiple vendor relationships. Health systems need to find a way out of this conundrum. In Chapter 6, we provide a detailed assessment of the technology provider landscape and have recommended strategies to tap into innovative solutions.

Key Takeaways and Action Steps

1. The journey begins with developing an enterprise vision and readiness assessment for digital transformation. Digital transformation needs sponsorship at the highest levels of the organization. It is a cross-functional business initiative that requires organizational and cultural change supported by new and innovative digital technologies.
2. Digital transformation is IT enabled, though not necessarily IT led. CIOs who lead digital transformation must take pains to ensure that enterprise-level digital transformation is not seen as an IT initiative. Ensure the involvement and buy-in of essential stakeholders, starting with the CEO of the enterprise. Consider setting up a digital transformation office with the authority to drive cross-functional initiatives.
3. Digital transformation leaders must gather input from as many sources as possible before committing to a path forward. They must seek input through internal surveys, site visits with peer group health systems, benchmarks from other sectors through technology partners and analysts, and their own research.
4. While recognizing the different phases of a digital transformation journey, adopt an agile approach to executing the digital roadmap by leveraging existing investments and departmental successes to show progress in the near-term.

5. Make extensive use of design tools such as journey maps to gain a deep understanding of customer needs. Prioritize the rollout of initiatives in alignment with overall enterprise objectives.
6. The technology solution landscape for an enterprise-level digital solution is maturing, and no single platform can meet all the digitalization needs of healthcare enterprises. Be prepared to take risks with digital health innovation and be ready to fail fast and safe.
7. Retreat idea: Gather a group of cross-functional stakeholders, including front-line caregivers, to conduct a journey-mapping exercise with help from an external facilitator to identify gaps that can be addressed through a digital front door application.

THIRTY-SECOND AGILE CONSULT

Do you have a digital transformation roadmap? If so, who owns it?

Chapter 4

Ensuring Strong Foundations

Digital transformation leaders might be tempted to skip this chapter, but it is important that all executives have a firm understanding of the foundations that enable digital transformation. We will not do an overly complex analysis of technology but hope to describe just enough so that health systems can understand the potential impact of technology infrastructure on digital transformation.

We barely notice how our smartphones respond to the slightest touch with hardly any time between request and response. The reality is that this seamless experience is enabled through a complex interplay between hundreds and thousands of backend applications, integration points, and digital infrastructure components, orchestrated to deliver the experience at the front end to the end user. Similarly, digital health requires a strong technology foundation to deliver seamless experiences. It requires robust processing power and networking infrastructure, data privacy and security, data management and interoperability, and more. Health systems are often burdened by decades of underinvestment and technical debt, which must be addressed as part of digital transformation. Being a digitally enabled organization requires a whole new way of working, where a deep understanding of concepts like agile, IT service management (ITSM), and technology business management (TBM) is already assumed in the emerging competitive landscape.

Data Ownership and Data Management

The use of patient data in emerging models of digital health innovation raises a basic question: Who owns the data?

The answer to this question was made clear by the Centers for Medicare and Medicaid Services (CMS) in early 2019.* CMS administrator Seema Verma went on record to state that healthcare consumers own their data, calling it an "epic misunderstanding" among healthcare providers and technology companies, specifically EHR vendors, who had evidently thought otherwise until then. A proposed 800-page ruling[†] by the Department of Health and Human Resources (HHS) aims to advance interoperability, specifically targeting healthcare programs administered by the CMS such as the Medicare fee-for-service program, Medicare Advantage program, Medicaid managed care organizations, and several others that account for a significant percentage of the overall healthcare spending in the United States. The HHS rule focuses on providing patients unfettered and no-cost access to their medical records to enable them to make informed healthcare decisions. Ironically, healthcare consumers have neither access to their personal medical information (not without jumping through

---

* "Speech: Remarks by Administrator Seema Verma at the 2019 HIMSS Conference." CMS.gov. February 12, 2019. Accessed December 13, 2019. www.cms.gov/newsroom/press-releases/speech-remarks-administrator-seema-verma-2019-himss-conference.

† "CMS Interoperability and Patient Access Proposed Rule." CMS.gov. March 4, 2019. Accessed December 13, 2019. www.cms.gov/Center/Special-Topic/Interoperability/CMS-9115-P.pdf.

many hoops) nor the ability to monetize it. The proposed HHS ruling covers health insurance companies, acknowledging that claims and encounter data sitting in payer systems can provide enrollees with a more complete picture of their medical history. The intent of the ruling is to allow healthcare consumers to have the data follow them around as they move from provider to provider or payer to payer. In addition, the ruling requires all data to be exposed through standard application programming interfaces (APIs) so that the developer community can build user-friendly applications to potentially help consumers access their data through devices and applications of their choice. In simple terms, API-led connectivity facilitates decentralized access to data and capabilities through reusable bits of code that eliminate the need to develop unique point-to-point connectors, which are complex and expensive to maintain.

The HHS ruling also addresses related issues, including data blocking and price transparency for healthcare procedures and outcomes. While the ruling goes into exhaustive detail on a number of topics, including data blocking and cybersecurity, here is how the ruling could impact three broad stakeholder categories in the healthcare ecosystem.

Patients: Providing patients with access to their own medical information is a giant step toward improved healthcare outcomes, not least because an informed consumer is in a better position to manage their own healthcare. However, the lack of a unique patient identifier, which hinders patient data matching, and the lack of standardization, especially at the semantic layer ("speaking the same language"), are significant challenges to implementing the interoperability vision outlined in the HHS ruling. In addition, patient data may not be up to date.

Clinicians and hospitals: Ensuring patients have ready access to their medical records, regardless of where they may have received care, is one of the key goals behind the HHS ruling. Due to the fragmented nature of the healthcare sector and the traditional lack of cooperation between providers and payers, when it comes to sharing data, this is a significant challenge today. Still, some organizations, such as Premera Blue Cross in Washington, have found creative solutions by partnering with a local health information exchange (HIE). The HIE aggregates patient medical information across the state and makes it available through a single API. Premera aggregates the data into its member database and makes it accessible to providers so that members are instantly recognized whenever they present their insurance card at any provider location.

Payers: The HHS ruling requires health plans to make their member health information available to members seamlessly as they change providers, plans, and employers. Here again, Premera's model could be an example of how to accomplish this by partnering with a local HIE so that the information is readily accessible by members and their healthcare providers at any time. Despite issues with semantic interoperability, the ability to interpret and present claims and member data in provider workflows in a seamless way is a win for payers.

Health plans and health systems are the custodians of healthcare data today. Health plans gather, store, and use the data to design health insurance products, price them appropriately, and offer a range of other benefits to their members. Health systems do the same, although the data sits in environments controlled and managed by their EHR vendors. Digital health innovators – with support from the CMS – have been in an ongoing battle with EHR vendors for several years for easier access to the data, while the CMS has been pushing to provide healthcare consumers with unfettered access to their personal medical histories.

Under the sponsorship of the Office of the National Coordinator of Health Systems (ONC), a growing number of tech firms and health systems have started signing the "interoperability pledge,"* committing themselves to collabo-

---

* "Interoperability Pledge." HealthIT.gov. Content last reviewed November 6, 2017. Accessed December 13, 2019. www.healthit.gov/topic/interoperability-pledge.

rate and share data – with the permission of the data owners – in order to bring about increased interoperability. The pledge requires participants to enable consumer access to data, adhere to national interoperability standards, and refrain from data-blocking practices.

In response to these pressures, the custodians of the data are opening up access and enabling the acceleration of innovation. A slew of collaboration initiatives points to the inexorable shift of data away from walled gardens and tightly controlled environments into the world of free markets. Apple has had remarkable success in giving iOS users access to health records from over 100 participating hospitals and health systems. Users, in turn, can share the data with their healthcare providers and others. In response, a group of healthcare institutions and technology providers has launched an open-source initiative titled CommonHealth* to let Android users gain access to medical records. The initiative will dramatically increase the number of consumers who will have access to their medical records, essentially replicating Apple's model.

For their part, EHR vendors, who have been targets of criticism for creating walled gardens around patient data, are progressively opening up access to patient health records in their custody. Allscripts, a health IT company, has opened up access† to its EHR system to Apple, enabling patients from hospitals using the Allscripts platform to access their records over their iOS devices. Epic has launched a massive data

---

* Donovan, Fred. "CommonHealth Enables Android Users to Share EHR with Health Apps." HIT Infrastructure. September 9, 2019. Accessed January 31, 2020. https://hitinfrastructure.com/news/commonhealth-enables-android-users-to-sh are-ehr-with-health-apps.

† Slabodkin, Greg. "Allscripts Offers Apple Health Records to Enable Patient Data Access." *Health Data Management.* August 29, 2019. Accessed December 13, 2019. www.healthdatamanagement.com/news/allscripts-offers-apple-health-recor ds-to-enable-patient-data-access.

compilation effort,* entitled Cosmos, to aggregate over 20 million patient medical records from providers in a participation agreement designed to make the data pool available for analysis in improving care decisions. A group of six of the largest technology firms signed a pledge† in 2019 to remove barriers for the adoption of technology to improve interoperability.

A growing trend in consumer data protection has been emerging legislation such as the General Data Protection Regulation (GDPR)‡ in Europe and the California Consumer Privacy Act (CCPA).§ There is growing consumer activism in general about data ownership and data use rights. Consumer data sourced from public sources have long been governed by restrictions on use. For instance, notwithstanding the current excitement about social determinants of health as strong predictors of health and wellness, healthcare enterprises have to be careful about how they incorporate third-party data on, say, a patient's criminal history, into electronic health records, or vice versa. The use of such data for making assessments about health risks may have direct consequences on a patient's cost and access to care. Ongoing concerns about the reckless use of consumer data by big tech firms have also highlighted the need for healthcare to ensure that data is ethically sourced before it is used in a clinical setting.

Patient medical information is being set free so that their rightful owners, i.e., consumers, can access and share it freely. The unlocking of patient data is leading us to a future when

---

* Bazzoli, Fred. "Epic to Gather Records of 20 Million Patients for Medical Research." *Health Data Management.* August 28, 2019. Accessed December 13, 2019. www.healthdatamanagement.com/news/epic-to-gather-records-of-20-million-patients-for-medical-research.

† "Open Letter by the Information Technology Industry Council." Accessed December 13, 2019. www.itic.org/dotAsset/efa935d2-743e-47ab-afdc-6ac1f4e1fd90.pdf.

‡ "General Data Protection Regulation." Accessed December 13, 2019. https://gdpr-info.eu/.

§ US State of California. *Assembly Bill No. 375.* June 29, 2018. Accessed December 13, 2019. https://leginfo.legislature.ca.gov/faces/billTextClient.xhtml?bill_id=201720180AB375.

healthcare will be a vastly improved experience with superior outcomes. However, there will be guardrails around consumer access to personal health records.

The ONC is trying to lubricate the free flow of data through a proposed Trusted Exchange Framework and Common Agreement (TEFCA) that will promote data interoperability among qualified health information networks. The ONC's moves are akin to forging a master digital key to unlock patient medical records at a national level. The ONC has even selected an official partner* – the Sequoia Project – to promote interoperability. While the ONC's proposed changes are yet to pass legislation as of writing, the significant outcome of these unlocking efforts will be a new wave of digital health innovation that will put the time, place, and mode of care delivery increasingly in the hands of healthcare consumers. However, the ONC has also rung a warning bell[†] against unregulated use of the data by third-party apps. Several medical associations have also raised the alarm[‡] about potential invasions of privacy arising from patients unwittingly granting access to their data to third parties. The ONC has highlighted likely undesirable effects, including the possibility of misuse of the data by insurance companies, employers, and others who may use the information to discriminate against consumers. These are valid concerns. Those of us who willingly signed away our data rights to big tech firms – who in turn unwittingly handed them off to malicious actors (recall Facebook and Cambridge

---

* "ONC Awards the Sequoia Project a Cooperative Agreement for the Trust Exchange Framework and Common Agreement to Support Advancing Nationwide Interoperability of Electronic Health Information." HHS.gov. September 3, 2019. Accessed December 13, 2019. www.hhs.gov/about/news/2019/09/03/onc-awards-the-sequoia-project-cooperative-agreement.html.

[†] Cohen, Jessica Kim. "Rucker: ONC Working on App Privacy with Congress, White House." *Modern Healthcare*. August 21, 2019. Accessed December 13, 2019. www.modernhealthcare.com/politics-policy/rucker-onc-working-app-privacy-congress-white-house.

[‡] Singer, Natasha. "When Apps Get Your Medical Data, Your Privacy May Go with It." *The New York Times*. September 3, 2019. Accessed December 13, 2019. www.nytimes.com/2019/09/03/technology/smartphone-medical-records.html.

Analytica) – will appreciate the need to slow down and ensure there are adequate guardrails to protect against misuse of personal medical information. Indeed, the horse may have already left the barn. Those among us who voluntarily uploaded our DNA data on open platforms may have compromised not just ourselves but our extended families as well. For every Golden State Killer who was nailed by a relative's DNA data,* there are likely some anonymous souls who have been targeted inappropriately due to their identities being compromised by a relative's online DNA record.

What we see now is a shift of control of patient data from one custodian to another, namely, from the health system to a technology provider or from one technology provider to another. The rightful owners of the data, namely, consumers, are gaining access through many of these arrangements, such as Apple's Health app, and will have the ability to direct the data to any platform or service they believe will help them with their healthcare goals (even though only around half of all patients have electronic access to their records† today and a large percentage of those don't look at them even once a year).

Even arrangements in which consumers do not gain access to their data may benefit them indirectly. Epic's Cosmos program may spur medical research that leads to breakthrough insights for improved care. Allscripts' data-sharing agreement with Apple unlocks hitherto inaccessible data from the EHR

---

* Kolata, Gina and Heather Murphy. "The Golden State Killer Is Tracked Through a Thicket of DNA, and Experts Shudder." *The New York Times*. April 27, 2018. Accessed December 13, 2019. www.nytimes.com/2018/04/27/health/dna-privacy-golden-state-killer-genealogy.html.
† US Department of Health and Human Services, Office of the National Coordinator for Health Information Technology. *Trends in Individuals' Access, Viewing and Use of Online Medical Records and Other Technology for Health Needs: 2017-2018*, by Vaishali Patel and Christian Johnson, ONC Data Brief No. 48. May 2019. Accessed December 13, 2019. www.healthit.gov/sites/default/files/page/2019-05/Trends-in-Individuals-Access-Viewing-and-Use-of-Online-Medical-Records-and-Other-Technology-for-Health-Needs-2017-2018.pdf.

system and hands it over to consumers. The many industry collaborations underway, such as the recently announced partnership* between Mayo Clinic and Google, could result in breakthroughs in clinical insights that could benefit the broader population. The ONC's TEFCA initiative – if it becomes law – will significantly enhance innovation and improvements in quality of care by enabling the free flow of patient data across the nation.

The one thing missing from all of these efforts is clarity on how much consumers can control how their data will be used in all these arrangements. In that sense, we are not in a free market for patient medical data, certainly not one where the consumer not only decides whom to share it with, but also how much to charge for access. But then, maybe we are not ready for a free market for patient data, and perhaps we never will be. This may not be entirely a bad thing, as long as the emerging data-sharing arrangements bring about improvements in patient experience and care quality while reducing costs of care.

The unlocking of patient data is leading us to a future when healthcare will be delivered at a time, place, and mode of the consumer's choosing. Consumers today can easily conduct financial transactions, such as moving money between different banks, thanks to the SWIFT† messaging system that is now used by over 11,000 banks and other financial institutions globally. So why can't we do it in healthcare? John Glaser, former CIO at Partners HealthCare, points out that healthcare data is much more complex than financial transaction data, and there is much less alignment among various players in the

---

* Ross, Casey. "Google, Mayo Clinic Strike Sweeping Partnership on Patient Data." *STAT.* September 10, 2019. Accessed December 13, 2019. www.statnews.com/201 9/09/10/google-mayo-clinic-partnership-patient-data/.

† Glaser, John. "What Banking Can Teach Health Care About Handling Customer Data." *Harvard Business Review.* October 14, 2019. Accessed December 13, 2019. https://hbr.org/2019/10/what-banking-can-teach-health-care-about-handling-c ustomer-data.

healthcare ecosystem. However, he argues that by concentrating on a few focused and highly impactful forms of interoperability, we may be able to achieve significant progress with data interoperability in healthcare.

Commercial use of deidentified patient and member data serves an essential purpose, namely, to enable and accelerate innovation in care delivery models that will ultimately benefit healthcare consumers through better outcomes and lower costs of care. Allowing digital health innovators and researchers access to the data enables them to apply advanced analytical tools to gain insights that can drive innovation in care delivery, manage population health, and a host of other things. Entities like Highmark are coming up with creative constructs to unlock the data and open it up for research and innovation – for a price.

Data Integration and Interoperability

The recent pandemic exposed significant gaps in this area that have magnified the need for investment and oversight. In 2018, a collective of seven hospital groups led by the American Hospital Association published a state-of-the-union report* on that most vexing of problems in healthcare information technology: interoperability. Despite the billions in taxpayer-funded incentives to facilitate a near-total EHR penetration among the nation's healthcare providers, interoperability between the numerous proprietary technology platforms remains an unfinished business (exacerbated by the tolls for access to data residing in proprietary systems).

The report made a case for interoperability (patient empowerment, improved care coordination, enhanced data

---

* American Hospital Association. *Sharing Data, Saving Lives: The Hospital Agenda for Interoperability.* January 2019. Accessed December 13, 2019. www.aha.org/sys tem/files/2019-01/Report01_18_19-Sharing-Data-Saving-Lives_FINAL.pdf.

quality, and healthcare outcomes) and highlighted barriers to technical interoperability (system-to-system data exchange) and semantic interoperability (common vocabulary across systems) as distinct but related challenges. The report concluded that interoperability has been partly achieved and is working well in some, but not all, settings. Data silos and the lack of interoperability were identified as the biggest challenges to digital transformation.

The architects of the Affordable Care Act* and the Health Information Technology for Economic and Clinical Health Act† of 2010 failed to recognize the crucial importance of interoperability. Belatedly, the 21st Century Cures Act‡ of 2016 turned the focus on the issue, and the ONC took up the cause in earnest, releasing a document§ in 2018 outlining a 10-year vision to achieve an interoperable health IT infrastructure. The ONC also set up an Interoperability Standards Advisory group to coordinate input from industry stakeholders.

To promote data exchange among providers, a number of regional health information exchanges were also set up. To facilitate data interoperability among the HIEs, the HHS released a set of guidelines with TEFCA¶ in 2018.

---

* "Affordable Care Act (ACA)." HealthCare.gov. Accessed December 13, 2019. www.healthcare.gov/glossary/affordable-care-act/.

† *HITECH Act Enforcement Interim Final Rule.* June 16, 2017. Accessed December 13, 2019. www.hhs.gov/hipaa/for-professionals/special-topics/hitech-act-enforcement-interim-final-rule/index.html.

‡ "21st Century Cures Act." FDA.gov. March 29, 2018. Accessed December 13, 2019. www.fda.gov/regulatory-information/selected-amendments-fdc-act/21st-century-cures-act.

§ Office of the National Coordinator for Health Information Technology. 2015. *Connecting Health and Care for the Nation: A Shared Nationwide Interoperability Roadmap.* A Shared Nationwide Interoperability Roadmap, Washington, DC: The Office of the National Coordinator for Health Information. https://www.healthit.gov/sites/default/files/hie-interoperability/nationwide-interoperability-roadmap-final-version-1.0.pdf.

¶ HealthIT.gov. 2019. *Trusted Exchange Framework and Common Agreement.* April 19. Accessed December 13, 2019. www.healthit.gov/topic/interoperability/trusted-exchange-framework-and-common-agreement.

Private sector efforts to promote interoperability have included two major initiatives, CommonWell* and Carequality,† enabling thousands of providers to connect through one of two major EHR platforms, Epic and Cerner. The Argonaut Project,‡ launched by the HL7 standards organization, promotes the use of Fast Health Interoperability Resources§ (FHIR) for standardizing data formats that can be used by APIs that connect disparate IT systems. Google has launched an alpha version of a healthcare API,¶ an ambitious effort to unify different standards into a single connectivity solution, albeit with the purpose of enabling access to the Google Cloud platform and applications.

Healthcare is now awash in traditional and emerging data sources. The two biggest challenges in using data from multiple sources are interoperability and identity matching. Even as technical interoperability challenges are being addressed through industry models such as FHIR, the issue of semantic interoperability is far from solved. This is at the core of identity matching, complicated further by the fact that there is no universal patient identifier today. However, many of the larger consumer data providers have developed proprietary algorithms for identity matching to varying degrees of accuracy, albeit in the narrow context of omni-channel marketing.

A few years back, there was great excitement around the data generated from smart sensors and wearables. The Internet of Things (IoT) was all the rage, with analyst firm Gartner predicting that 8.4 billion connected "things" would be in use

---

* CommonWell Health Alliance. Accessed December 13, 2019. www.commonwel-lalliance.org/.

† Carequality. Accessed December 13, 2019. https://carequality.org/.

‡ "Main Page: Welcome to the Argonaut Project." Health Level Seven International. Last edited June 11, 2019. Accessed December 13, 2019. https://argonautwiki.hl7.org/Main_Page.

§ HL7. 2019. *FHIR Overview*. November 1. Accessed December 13, 2019. www.hl7.org/fhir/overview.html.

¶ "Cloud Healthcare API." Google Cloud. Accessed December 13, 2019. https://cloud.google.com/healthcare/.

in 2017.* What we have seen since is that there is not that much value in data; in addition to issues with data quality, sufficiency, and interoperability, simply being able to capture transactional metrics with smart sensors and wearables does not create tremendous value, unless we are able to obtain actionable information by using advanced analytics or artificial intelligence (AI).

As new data sources come online and non-traditional players enter the market, the need for data liquidity for real-time access to a comprehensive view of patients will drive interoperability efforts. Related challenges, including latencies in aggregating real-time data from devices into a centralized repository, data management on cloud and on-premises environments, ensuring the veracity of parties involved in data exchange, and semantic interoperability, will become front and center in the pursuit of data liquidity. The growing acceptance of FHIR as the standard for exchanging health information electronically now means that industry participants can focus on adding more content to the data model. Finally, harnessing the vast amounts of data from IoT devices means that networks must be upgraded to 5G for real-time analysis and insights at the point of care. To address this issue of processing power and speed, there is a growing trend toward edge computing, which allows device data to be analyzed at the edges of the network instead of being transferred to a central repository for aggregation and analysis.

With the rise of API-led connectivity as an important enabler for digital transformation, Interoperability is cool again. For the past few years, data interoperability has been the poster child for lack of progress in digital health innovation. The CMS' Interoperability and Patient Access

---

* Van Der Meulen, Rob. "Gartner Says 8.4 Billion Connected 'Things' Will Be in Use in 2017, Up 31 Percent from 2016." *Gartner.* February 7, 2017. Accessed December 13, 2019. www.gartner.com/en/newsroom/press-releases/2017-02-07-g artner-says-8-billion-connected-things-will-be-in-use-in-2017-up-31-percent-from-2016.

final rule, announced in early 2020, delivers on the promise to "put patients first, giving them access to their health information when they need it and, in a way they can best use it." The CMS's final rule accelerates innovation through the removal of information blocking practices and enables IT systems enable access to the underlying data through a set of APIs. The emergence of the API-led app economy is a fundamental driver for technology-led innovation in healthcare.

In the face of competitive pressures, healthcare enterprises are increasingly concerned about speed and agility in creating digital experiences for patients and caregivers. The ability to gain access to the data through reusable APIs significantly improves developer productivity, enabling CIOs to achieve more with the same resources. Developers need no longer worry about changes in the underlying data structures. They can rely instead on APIs to do the job for them and focus more on orchestrating the data to compose new applications rapidly.

Digital transformation initiatives are commonly associated with new and digitally enabled patient experiences. Most users of digital front door applications do not really know (or care) how the data behind the scenes is aggregated and orchestrated to deliver the experiences. Aside from intuitive user experience and interface design, the real key to delivering on the promise of the experience is presenting the data in real-time at the experience layer. Consider this: For a patient trying to get a physician appointment through a patient app, the app has to be able to connect in the back end with a provider directory, use an AI algorithm to identify the right match, access a calendar for available spots, and link it to the nearest physical location for the patient. APIs that access data from multiple back end systems enable the experience just described. What is more, a digitally enabled scheduling function eliminates much of the manual effort, wait times, and frustration for patients that is the current state at most hospitals and health systems. APIs are at the heart of enabling such experiences.

Healthcare IT environments operate with hundreds of connectors, developed on multiple data exchange standards, performing the integration function. With the increasing pace of innovation, IT functions are being required to democratize the access to data and standardize the means of access so that a broad range of developers, within and outside the organization, can quickly and easily compose applications with minimal effort on back end integrations.

The emergence of API management platforms (distinct from integration gateways) that control, provision, and monitor access to the library of APIs across the enterprise, has advanced API-led development. With new data sources emerging every day, including non-healthcare data such as social determinants, and unstructured data, such as images, having an API-led integration strategy and an effective way to manage the APIs has become a priority for healthcare technology leaders.

Consulting firm PwC's survey* of over 300 CEOs across the globe indicated that 2019 was the year enterprises expected to extract value from data: the data that enterprises value most? – Consumer data, which includes demographic, lifestyle, and health data. Traditionally, consumer data has been within the purview of major established firms in the space, such as Experian and Acxiom, who have built vast data repositories by aggregating, organizing, and monetizing data from a large number of public and commercial sources to help marketers target their audiences in evermore refined ways.

There is a gold rush for data as marketers, healthcare technologists, and medical practitioners look for data-led strategies to drive revenues, reduce costs, and improve healthcare outcomes. However, healthcare professionals are less than

---

* "Data Trust Pulse Survey." PwC. Accessed December 13, 2019. www.pwc.com/us/en/services/consulting/cybersecurity/data-optimization/pulse-survey.html.

satisfied with the results so far from their traditional sources of patient medical information such as electronic health records. The issues range from a lack of data to too much and not enough insights, the usability of data, and challenges with enterprise data management, to name but a few. Consumer data adds a level of complexity to the mix while promising incremental benefits.

Today, most use cases for consumer data lie in marketing. Pharmaceutical companies, which spend billions of dollars in advertising, have used consumer data for a long time to define target audiences and direct their media spend. Large health plans, and to a lesser extent, health systems, have also used consumer data for similar purposes. However, we look at it, the stakes are big, going by the vast amounts of money that data providers make by licensing their data to healthcare companies.

As the healthcare sector accelerates its move to value-based care (the HHS has proposed* shifting a quarter of all health-care payments to accountable care models, though actual progress toward alternative payment models has been much slower than anticipated), healthcare enterprises are looking to deploy data and insights as primary tools for population health management, precision medicine, evidence-based drug pricing, and more. Advanced analytics and AI tools that require not just vast amounts of data but also diverse data sets for training and refining the algorithms are looking to consumer data for new insights about healthcare consumers.

As newer sources of data become available from the proliferation of smart devices and digitization of consumer-facing processes, there will be a greater need to understand health-care consumers from an omni-channel perspective and serve them accordingly.

---

* Azar II, Alex M. "Remarks on Primary Care to the American Medical Association." HHS.gov. April 22, 2019. Accessed December 13, 2019. www.hhs.go v/about/leadership/secretary/speeches/2019-speeches/remarks-primary-care-am erican-medical-association.html.

As healthcare data breaches continue unabated* and technology vendors get ensnared† in attempts by hackers to indirectly infiltrate client systems, what may seem like gold to marketers may seem like risk-bearing assets to the health-care C-suite, stung by penalties for HIPAA‡ violations several years in a row. As data sources and data types increase, the lines have blurred between what was traditionally considered consumer data and what is now considered protected per-sonal information. Acquiring and deploying consumer data in healthcare enterprises has now become a question of trust. And that trust is engendered not just through robust data secu-rity practices but also data privacy policies, which now include strict compliance requirements with the EU's data protection regulation GDPR and the recently passed consumer privacy rules in California, CCPA.§

In the next few years, we will see dramatic changes in the world of healthcare data. Consumers will gain control of exist-ing data about themselves and enrich it with data generated from their smart devices as well as their lifestyle and habits. They will also share it selectively with their healthcare provid-ers and others (perhaps for some meaningful compensation; however, consumers looking to trade data for cash must also

---

* Cohen, Jessica Kim. "Healthcare Breaches Reported in March Exposed Data of 883,000 People." Modern Healthcare. April 12, 2019. Accessed December 13, 2019. www.modernhealthcare.com/technology/healthcare-breaches-reported-march-exposed-data-883000-people.

† O'Flaherty, Kate. "Breaking Down The Wipro Breach -- And What It Means for Supply Chain Security." Forbes. April 16, 2019. Accessed December 13, 2019. www.forbes.com/sites/kateoflahertyuk/2019/04/16/breaking-down-the-wipro-breach-and-what-it-means-for-supply-chain-security/.

‡ "Health Information Privacy." HHS.gov. Accessed December 13, 2019. www.hhs.gov/hipaa/index.html.

§ "California Consumer Privacy Act (CCPA)." State of California Department of Justice. Accessed December 13, 2019. https://oag.ca.gov/privacy/ccpa.

be aware that there are limited protections under law from unintended consequences of secondary use).*

For healthcare enterprises, emerging data such as genomic data and social determinants of health will increasingly drive medical decisions in addition to core EHR data. The use of consumer data, which drives many other sectors such as banking and finance, has barely scratched the surface in healthcare. The value of consumer data is evident in recent multi-billion dollar acquisitions of Acxiom by media giant IPG† and Epsilon by Publicis.‡ As consumerism gains ground in healthcare, healthcare enterprises and their data providers will increasingly collaborate to drive the digital transformation of healthcare.

A foundational requirement of digital transformation and digital health innovation is that enterprises have to get the data right. In the last decade, enterprises mostly committed to traditional on-premises data warehouses (and later, data lakes), where data sets get aggregated, mapped, and translated. Most enterprises have deployed vast amounts of expert resources such as database administrators (DBAs) to manage data quality issues. The emerging practice is to migrate data to cloud environments, such as Amazon Web Services or Azure, and place data quality in the hands of users of the data, such as nurses and clinicians, who have a much better appreciation of the accuracy and relevance of the data and can address data quality issues further upstream than the DBAs or data scientists. This emerging approach is increasingly the preferred option for large health systems looking to leverage advanced analytics

---

* Klosowski, Thorin. *What to Consider Before Trading Your Health Data for Cash.* December 2, 2019. Accessed January 29, 2020. www.nytimes.com/2019/11/27/smarter-living/wirecutter/what-to-consider-before-trading-your-health-data-for-cash.html?smid=nytcore-ios-share.

† Acxiom. *Acxiom Marketing Solutions Joins IPG Family of Companies.* October 1, 2018. Accessed January 27, 2020. www.acxiom.com/news/acxiom-marketing-solutions-joins-ipg-family-of-companies/.

‡ "Publicis Groupe to Acquire Epsilon." Publicis Groupe. April 14, 2019. Accessed December 13, 2019. www.publicisgroupe.com/en/news/press-releases/publicis-groupe-to-acquire-epsilon.

tools such as AI and machine learning, which we cover in Chapter 5. However, the challenge of data management continues to grow, with newer data sources emerging every day.

The ideal state for all participants in the healthcare data ecosystem is to have seamlessly connected, vendor-neutral platforms that allow a free flow of data and information across healthcare IT systems. However, "The business case for interoperability lies in being very targeted about the transactions," says John Glaser, former CIO of Partners HealthCare.

While technology-led innovation in healthcare continues to leverage vast and diverse emerging data sources, EHR systems, designed primarily for documenting clinical data for billing for healthcare services, remain critically important for population health management and precision medicine. However, EHR data alone is no longer sufficient in an era of digital health. As innovative start-ups and large technology firms build applications running on robust cloud infrastructure that aggregate and analyze data using advanced technologies, EHRs will lose their position as the primary data source in digital health innovation.

Significant progress has been made by the HL7 organization's FHIR standards for data exchange, and healthcare is steadily eliminating multiple competing standards with an API-based approach to integration. This reduces transaction costs and accelerates innovation and development cycles. With increased interoperability, health systems that default to their EHR vendor – in order to avoid integration costs for advanced capabilities such as digital and AI from other technology providers – will find easy-to-deploy alternatives that are zero-cost and friction-free from a data integration perspective.

Daniel Barchi, CIO of New York–Presbyterian Hospital, believes that interoperability is not a technology challenge per se:

> Data is certainly an outstanding tool for improving our operations financially, from an efficiency point of view and from a clinical point of view. When people

> say it is hard to get data out of systems, be they
> financial systems or billing systems or clinical sys-
> tems, it is sort of lazy second-hand for acknowledg-
> ing that this work is challenging.

He further says:

> We should spend more time actually drilling down
> into what conclusions we want to draw, what data
> sets we need to get that information from, and how
> we take the right steps, rather than simply saying it is
> hard to get data out of the system. It is not a technol-
> ogy challenge around aggregating data or deciding
> where to store it. It is about who has access to it and
> how we make that access readily available to the
> researchers and the clinicians who need it.

Despite the significant progress made around interoperability
in the past few years, there is still a nagging sense that it will
remain a gnarly problem for some time to come. Achieving
population health objectives and personalized medicine requires
multiple stakeholders in the delivery of care – namely, providers, payers, and pharmaceutical/biotechnology companies – to
collaborate and share data. We are a long way away from this
end state. The reasons are many, including a history of mistrust between stakeholders on opposite sides of the table and
a new zeal for treating data as a source of competitive advantage. However, as Dr. Toby Cosgrove, former CEO of Cleveland
Clinic, puts it, "As we move towards capitation and value, data
sharing between payers and providers will improve."

Security and Privacy

"We're thinking about cybersecurity all the time," says John
Kravitz, CIO of Geisinger Health. Cybersecurity is one of the

top three priorities for any business leader today, even more so in healthcare, which has been the target of repeated cyberattacks and ransomware demands. Data security is at the forefront of every healthcare CIO's mind, and there is a constant effort to improve cybersecurity defenses and surveillance techniques.

In 2019, there were over 1,400 data breaches in healthcare, a 17 percent increase over 2018.* Ransomware and phishing attacks continue to be at the top of the list of causes for breaches, as phishing attempts become increasingly sophisticated.

While the formalized role of the chief information security officer has only emerged in the last 20 years, the adoption of information security practices has accelerated significantly in the past five years. CEOs and CIOs are acutely aware that a single data breach could cost them their job and tarnish the reputation of the enterprise. In a digital future, the stakes are even higher, as healthcare enterprises collaborate increasingly digitally with external stakeholder groups and a breach with a business associate can compromise the information security of the enterprise.

The healthcare industry takes care of people usually in the most difficult time of their lives and is the steward of data for very vulnerable people. Breaking the trust between clinician and patient by being poor stewards of security and inadvertently exposing their data is a worst-case scenario. Health systems have made an implicit promise to take excellent care not only of patients' health, but of their privacy and security as well.

Healthcare has become the highest-value target among hackers for a few reasons. Healthcare is woefully behind other industries when it comes to technology. Cybersecurity is no exception. There is a strong demand for healthcare data in

---

* Garrity, Mackenzie. "Number of Data Breaches Jumped 17% in 2019: 3 Things to Know." January 29, 2020. Accessed February 03, 2020. www.beckershospitalr eview.com/cybersecurity/number-of-data-breaches-jumped-17-in-2019-3-things-to-know.html.

the black markets because healthcare data is relatively easy to obtain and contains numerous personal identity elements that enable identity theft and fraud. Healthcare data is also fragmented over numerous systems and devices, including technology solutions managed by business associates, making it easier to find vulnerability in the system.

As the number of end points for information systems increases, so do the vulnerabilities and the potential for data breach. Everything built in the digital era must therefore include robust cybersecurity. Given the high stakes with data security, cybersecurity hygiene is now a CEO-level issue for most organizations. Following the example of other sectors such as banking and finance, healthcare organizations should source or build their own 24/7 cybersecurity operations centers. Cybersecurity drills should be conducted regularly to include direct C-suite engagement. A multifactorial cybersecurity defense should be in place, and its effectiveness should be tested by unaffiliated third parties. A long-range plan should be reviewed twice annually to provide updates and make adjustments. Results of all testing and progress should be reported to the CEO and board of directors.

It is not a matter of if your organization will be breached, but when. The true test is around resiliency. How quickly are you aware you have been breached and how quickly do you resolve it?

Technical Debt and Infrastructure Readiness

"Making the foundational technology work enables you to build digital capability for the enterprise," says Nader Mherabi, CIO of NYU Langone Health. When Mherabi says "making the foundational technology work," he is referring not only to the need for a robust infrastructure but also to the technical debt that prevents many health systems from accelerating their digital transformation programs. Technical debt refers to the accumulation of underinvestment and short-term fixes that eventually limit an enterprise's ability to grow. Technical debt creates an unfunded liability and inhibits the enterprise's ability to invest in new technologies for a digital future.

Most health systems operate with tight IT budgets that reflect the organization's view of IT as primarily a cost center. Considering that the bulk of the budget goes toward IT labor, infrastructure, and software renewal and maintenance costs, there is not much left for new initiatives. Notwithstanding the vast amounts of venture capital money pouring into digital health solutions, the reality is that the core transactional systems that run healthcare enterprises are far more critical to the smooth functioning of the organization, especially in a predominantly fee-for-service environment.* Part of the challenge for digital transformation, as well as the transformation to a value-based care model, is the challenge of technical debt. Undoing decades of suboptimal choices and under investments in information technology and integrating them into easy-to-use technology stacks is a big challenge for healthcare today. Here are some of the major components of technical debt in healthcare enterprises.

High Levels of Investment in Traditional Data Center Environments

At a time when a rapid transition to the cloud is almost a necessity for scale and speed, many health systems are left with high levels of investments in data centers that are yet to be amortized fully. One reason why traditional data centers will continue to play a significant role in IT environments is the need for high availability and high reliability of EHR systems in a patient care environment.

---

* Padmanabhan, Paddy. "Digital Transformation and the Law of Small Numbers." CIO. July 25, 2018. Accessed December 13, 2019. www.cio.com/article/3293056/digital-transformation-and-the-law-of-small-numbers.html.

Suboptimal Utilization of Significant Software Investments

Over the past decade, countless millions of dollars have gone into implementing costly EHR systems. Many early adopters of EHR systems are now looking at a steep price tag for upgrading and optimizing EHR platforms to take advantage of newer functionalities. The upgrades may be required to benefit from new digital features or solutions that are part of the vendor's product roadmap.

Siloed Data Repositories and Decentralized Analytics Initiatives

As the volume of data explodes and newer data sources become available, the challenge of data governance and analytics becomes increasingly complex. Even in organizations with centralized enterprise analytics functions, there are departmental initiatives that use siloed data repositories and custom-built algorithms to analyze the data.

The spaghetti of applications in a healthcare environment that are connected via point-to-point integration has made legacy applications costly to maintain and a major impediment to digital transformation. The emergence of API platforms that are built on frameworks of reusability can significantly reduce the costs of application maintenance and increase productivity by enabling developers to quickly spin up applications in response to fast-changing marketplace needs. Other areas such as compliance and enterprise IT security also carry significant technical debt and consume increasingly larger shares of IT budgets with each passing year.

"At NYU Langone Health, we have great leadership who really see IT, technology, and digital as great enablers, not just an expense but a strategic asset to propel the organization forward in its mission," says Nader Mherabi, CIO. For the past eight or nine years, his organization has been very focused on fixing the guts of technology and platform delivery. NYU Langone has standardized its EHR system across the enterprise so that all hospitals and ambulatory locations use one EHR and one common standardized workflow. That allows the enterprise to assess the same quality of care across all locations and ensure a consistently high-quality patient experience. The standardization also allows Mherabi to reduce the cost of maintenance for the technology. As a result of the standardization, he does not need an army of staff to maintain various workflows and is able to use the dollars saved to improve the patient or family experience through technology. He concludes, "If we are thoughtful about it, we don't have to spend a lot of money on just EHRs. The implementation of EHR costs money, but standardization is the key to controlling costs."

Mherabi summarizes well the challenge for corporate CIOs and technical debt. Every major transformation requires an upfront investment, which is often prohibitive in the context of a finite amount of discretionary funds. However, not all transformational initiatives need vast amounts of upfront investments. Selective investments that deliver near-term returns can be the building blocks for an enterprise-wide digital transformation. While enterprise data centers continue to run major workloads, newer workloads for digital health and analytics applications can be managed in the cloud in a gradual transition toward a hybrid cloud environment. The solution for point-to-point integration is to invest in a robust API platform that can standardize interfaces, supported by a common data model and interoperability standards such as FHIR. A center of excellence for advanced analytics with a small but highly qualified team of data scientists can take ownership for managing sophisticated analytical models and algorithms, ensure robust validation through a centrally governed training data set, and track model performance over time.

Technical debt can eventually limit an enterprise's ability to grow and seriously constrain the deployment of new digital experience platforms. Essential elements for implementing a digital platform include robust IT security, upgraded network infrastructure, cloud enablement, and unified communications, to name but a few. Given the financial and organizational constraints associated with large-scale IT infrastructure upgrades, health systems must carefully sequence the implementation of digital innovation roadmaps to keep the enterprise moving forward in the digital journey.

ITSM, Agile, and TBM

"Healthcare IT is 80 percent people, 15 percent process, and 5 percent technology," says Daniel Barchi of New York–Presbyterian Hospital. Many organizations are eager to jump right into digital transformation. When you consider the potential for impact and improvement, the reasons are clear. Using our agile digital transformation approach, it is possible to jump in, but digital transformation leaders will need to revisit the foundation for long-term success: culture. Within culture are the concepts and practical applications of service management, agile methods, and how to operate IT as a business. For long-term success, taking the time and resources to build out this operating model will pay dividends.

IT Service Management (ITSM)

IT service management is a highly regarded and accepted best practice IT operating model. ITSM is the implementation and management of quality IT services that meet the needs of the business. IT service management is performed by IT service providers through an appropriate mix of people, processes, and information technology. IT professionals should be expected to learn and utilize best practices to ensure desired business and clinical outcomes.

ITSM begins with strategy and then moves to service design, transition, and operations. Similar to the plan, do, study, act model that many professionals in healthcare have utilized, it is a complete circle wrapped around a continuous improvement model. Many health system IT organizations run without a formal operating model. Most IT organizations' operating models are based on how things have always been done, with a few modifications thrown in. Health systems need a robust and codified operating model to ensure IT is fully capable of executing digital transformation.

Consider the example of change management. Most IT organizations employ an informal model on how to make changes in the technology environment that relies on specific individuals with knowledge of how things work at that specific organization. When this person is not available, how does the organization handle the change? As organizations grow increasingly complex, it is no longer possible to count on just a small handful of individuals to handle change. With ITSM, the change model requires that the process be completely written out, and it includes checks and balances so that failures are avoided. There are specific steps an organization must take to make any change in a technical environment. There are formal reviews and specific processes for emergencies.

We recommend hiring a third party to complete an ITSM review and conduct a corresponding maturity model to identify gaps. Develop a plan to close those gaps and improve maturity. ITSM also has a professional certification capability, which Ed has deployed at multiple organizations with great success. For those specialized in advanced services, additional certifications are available. Organizations with mature ITSM programs have experienced significant reductions in major incidents.

Agile

Agile methodology is a specific approach to project management popularized in the field of software development. The process assists teams in responding to the unpredictability of software development and projects using incremental, iterative work sequences commonly referred to as "sprints." Agile projects also contain "scrums" (a framework for project management that emphasizes teamwork, accountability, and iterative progress toward a well-defined goal) and "scrum masters" or leaders. Agile has grown in popularity, and many digital-age companies such as Facebook and Spotify have adopted agile for their entire business operations. In Chapter 3, we described how agile principles can be applied for digital transformation.

Traditional companies are often static, siloed, and structurally hierarchical. Objectives and key results flow from the top down, with the C-suite leading all decisions. Strategic planning and controls are all linear. While the structure is stable, it is bureaucratic and slow. Agile organizations are a network of teams, often referred to as "teams of teams." These people-centric organizations operate in rapid, technology-enabled cycles (sprints), typically two weeks in length. What differentiates these companies is their ability to reconfigure strategy, structure, and processes. Agile organizations are flexible and fast at their core, enabling them to respond to market conditions or technology enhancements with velocity and finesse.

Compare two hospitals that want to launch a digital front door or a new patient-facing application. The traditional hospital spends weeks deciding on functionality and design. IT uses traditional project management approaches, and developers begin their work. Six months later, IT reveals its new product to the designers. Given the lapse of time, competing initiatives, preference changes, and misunderstanding, the product undergoes a redesign and will be late to market. The agile hospital conducts everything in two-week sprints, and there is a continuous dialogue between all parties. Sprints are an agile term to describe a set period of time in which specific work must be completed and made ready for review. Each sprint begins with a planning meeting, and there are daily huddles to review progress and obstacles. A minimally viable product is launched after two months, and adjustments are made and implemented every two weeks. The agile hospital goes live with its new application in three months, while the traditional hospital continues to be frustrated and misses an important opportunity.

Agile methods can benefit the entire company, not just software development and project management, and can complement a strong ITSM foundation to prepare for digital transformation.

Technology Business Management (TBM)

Technology business management is a value-management framework instituted by CIOs, CTOs, and other technology leaders. Founded on transparency of costs, consumption, and performance, TBM gives technology leaders and their business partners the facts they need to collaborate on business-aligned decisions. This framework can help organizations better understand technology value, increase collaboration, and allow for deeper insights into technology spending. Organizations that adopt this framework share anonymized data so that all contributors can benchmark against each other.

A simple example would be staffing. With TBM, organizations can benchmark themselves against others in a specific industry or by revenue, number of full-time employees, etc. The benchmark may show that the average organization has 1 network engineer per 200 nodes. To advocate for more network engineer resources, digital leaders can use the industry benchmark for comparison.

IT should be positioned as a strategic enabler for digital transformation. In the past, IT departments often had a lock on technology. Despite the ineffectiveness of such a model, business and clinical leaders had no alternative but to be frustrated and patient with slow progress. With the advent of personalized and cloud computing, this has all changed. Coupled with ITSM and agile, TBM allows IT organizations to reposition themselves to help lead digital transformation.

TBM can be the catalytic operating model that puts IT on par with all other parts of the organization. By adhering to the key themes of transparency and accountability, IT helps eliminate fences and reduce obstacles.

There are few healthcare IT organizations today that have been intentional when it comes to building a strong foundation. For digital transformation to be realized, leaders need to proactively develop a mature IT organization. Leveraging ITSM best practices, agile methods for operating, and transparency and accountability associated with TBM, healthcare organizations will be ready.

Key Takeaways and Action Steps

1. The pandemic has increased the need to rapidly assess and address data management, integration, and interoperability between systems.

2. Creating seamless digital experiences requires a complex interplay between hundreds and thousands of backend applications, integration points, and infrastructure components. Understand the readiness of the IT infrastructure components before rolling out a new digital health solution.

3. Technical debt from years of underinvestment in core infrastructure technologies must be addressed concurrently with digital transformation programs. Where possible, migrate to current technologies to ensure digital readiness. Infrastructure upgrades must be an essential component of the budgeting and planning process for digital roadmap implementation.

4. Data is foundational to the digital transformation of healthcare. Digital leaders and their technology partners must understand data ownership laws, protect the enterprise against data breaches, and implement robust data governance and data management practices. Digital

leaders must ensure that as data sources proliferate, the organization is able to quickly and easily aggregate and integrate the data and not be held back by interoperability challenges. Consider an API-led strategy to unlock the data from source systems and render than accessible to developers for accelerated innovation.

5. Ensure discipline and accountability by adopting agile methodologies and following best practices in ITSM and TBM.

6. Retreat idea: Conduct an assessment of your IT capabilities' maturity. Look specifically at best practice adoption, benchmarks, and operating models. Consider readiness for a move to agile methodology. Finalize the analysis and establish multi-year maturity goals to establish strong and flexible foundational capabilities.

30-SECOND AGILE CONSULT

What percentage of your organization's revenue goes to IT-related investments, and is it increasing or decreasing?

Chapter 5

Leveraging Maturing and Emerging Technologies

Technological advances in the past decade have provided health systems with enormously powerful tools to enhance productivity and increase convenience. Pandemic inspired advances in 2020 alone have doubled capabilities. Chapter 4 explained that a strong foundation is necessary to harness the power of new technologies to drive the digital health experiences of the future. Platform technologies in search, social, and e-Commerce have transformed the way we live and work. The giant technology companies that dominate these fields rely on robust underlying infrastructure just as traditional enterprises do. To compete in the digitally enabled competitive landscape, healthcare enterprises must harness new and emerging technologies alongside their legacy platforms. The prevailing technologies for digital transformation success in healthcare are cloud computing, voice recognition, advanced analytics, and artificial intelligence (AI). A handful of emerging technologies have significant potential for the future. Leaders must keep their eyes on all of these, anticipating the future.

Analytics, Machine Learning, and AI

"We're still in a gold rush phase of artificial intelligence in healthcare," says Daniel Barchi, CIO of New York–Presbyterian Hospital. As the practice of medicine moves from art to science, data becomes increasingly important. A tremendous amount of data about healthcare consumers comes from a vast and growing range of sources. The data provides the ability to bring science to the delivery of care as advanced analytical tools such as AI and machine learning discern insights from the data that can drive precision and personalized medicine. The increasing amount of data from an increasing number of sources is challenging to manage, but it also provides an opportunity to learn new things and make unprecedented predictions. Much is made of the potential for advanced analytics, but the vast majority of health systems are still deeply entrenched in retrospective analytics. Advanced analytics that provide predictive insights at the point of care and are integrated into the workflow of clinical decision support are still very much work in progress.

The shift toward value-based care and precision and personalized medicine implies the need for advanced analytics in healthcare delivery. Terms like "artificial intelligence," "machine learning," "deep learning," and "predictive analytics" are commonly used today by technology vendors as well as health systems. However, it remains difficult to separate the signal from the noise to make investment decisions to support advanced analytics initiatives. "With AI, you don't typically see a ton of results in the first six to twelve months," says Steve Miff, CEO of Parkland Center for Clinical Innovation (PCCI), a spin-off of Dallas-based Parkland Hospitals that leverages data science and social determinants of health to better support underserved populations across our communities. PCCI has been able to identify simple interventions involving basic lifestyle factors such as nutrition to reduce both the preterm births and costs of care.

There is limited information available on the scale of investment required to set up and run an advanced analytics program or the returns from such investments. There is an increasing volume and diversity of data sources and an increasing range of technology choices for implementing advanced analytics. Selecting the right tools and platforms is challenging due to the early stage of maturity of the entire industry. Finally, launching and managing an advanced analytics program requires not just investing in analytics and technology, but also effectively integrating analytical tools and insights into the clinical workflow in a closed-loop process that ensures accountability for sustained improvement. This can be a technological and organizational challenge.

To get a sense of how medical institutions are approaching advanced analytics, we researched the top 25 academic medical centers (AMCs) in the United States to understand what kind of AI initiatives they were investing in and how the initiatives were being funded. Here is what we found:

- Most leading AMCs in the United States have an advanced analytics program and are using machine learning, predictive analytics, and AI in some form. Key disease areas of focus are cancer, heart and lung conditions, sepsis, genetic anomalies, and asthma.
- A handful of institutions – University of Pittsburgh Medical Center, Icahn School of Medicine at Mount Sinai in New York, University of California (San Francisco), and Stanford University Medical Center – appear to be further along on advanced analytics and AI.
- Many institutions are investing in healthcare ecosystem collaborations to strengthen analytics programs. These include technology partnerships as well as data and research partnerships with the private and education sectors. Not surprisingly, partnerships within the same geographic region (e.g., Northern California) are common.

■ Public institutions, such as the Centers for Medicare and Medicaid Services and Centers for Disease Control and Prevention, are using big data analytics to predict disease outbreaks, reduce claims fraud, and advance medical research. All of them have strategic long-term partnerships with the healthcare and technology sectors for data, analytics, and cloud-computing capabilities.

■ Many AMCs have relied on grants to launch advanced analytics research. The grants have been made available from public sources (e.g., National Science Foundation) as well as private ones (e.g., Chan Zuckerberg Foundation).

In the midst of healthcare's digital transformation of key aspects of patient engagement and care management, the role of data, analytics, and AI is central to the organizational mission. However, it is easy to get caught up in one aspect or another when extolling (or decrying) the role of AI, while ignoring the near-term potential as well as the limitations of the technology.

How can AI play a role in healthcare today? AI applications cover a range of scenarios. AI can enable physicians to deliver better care through insights on individual patients as well as populations. It can be used to improve productivity and efficiency, for example, by automating routine tasks and using natural language processing (NLP) to analyze vast amounts of medical literature. It can accelerate research and advance new cures through faster drug discovery. As with most emerging technologies, the use case is important. What may be a high priority for an academic medical research institution may not be as important for the revenue cycle management function of a large hospital struggling to accelerate cash flow cycles.

With the emergence of cheap computing and storage infrastructure, AI technologies can analyze vast and diverse data sources, detecting and remediating the most common problems without human intervention. Purpose-built hardware solutions with built-in AI capabilities are becoming the norm in high-volume and time-sensitive operations that require running machine-learning algorithms on large data sets at low costs.

The notion of edge computing, a paradigm that takes analytics and AI to the edges of computing infrastructure, has lately become important in the context of the Internet of Things and smart devices. In healthcare, the proliferation of intelligent devices, in and out of hospital settings, has created many new opportunities. The emergence of smart medical devices allows us to create digital diaries that can log every minute and every second of a device's operation in the context of patient care. It is now possible to track a mobile device in a caregiver's hands as they make their way through a hospital floor, recording and analyzing everything from their precise location to their pace of walking, to the direction they are headed with the device. Extending it to outpatient or even home healthcare, intelligent devices that can analyze data at the end point and send it back to a backend system can save lives by reducing the time involved alerting caregivers to medical emergencies. This type of passive data gathering has given rise to the term "ambient computing", which is a way of gathering and contextualizing data in a non-obtrusive way so that caregivers can become more productive with their time and improve the overall quality of interactions and outcomes for patients.

To some, all of this may sound futuristic. However, the use cases and situations do not need to be complex or high risk in order to determine whether AI is suitable for a healthcare institution. The vast majority of AI use cases involve low-hanging fruit that automate routine and/or repetitive operations. AI can release humans from mundane tasks and enable them to work on more exciting and value-added tasks. In some industries with an acute shortage of skilled human resources such as healthcare, this may even be a necessity for long-term sustainability. As Daniel Barchi says, "At this point with artificial intelligence, the gold is not in the clinical side of healthcare.

The gold right now is on the back-office side of it." It is much easier to apply AI to a billing system to make predictions about which bills will or will not be approved by a payer or to look at documentation by a physician and see if it's going to pass muster. Today, artificial intelligence can do the basic robotic process automation work of reaching out to an insurance company, looking up information online, and aggregating data.

The use of AI technologies comes with responsibilities as well. AI can be a force for good or bad. Among the concerns, AI technologies by themselves may not have any inherent biases but may reflect the biases of the humans who design the systems, as well as the underlying data sets on which they are initially trained. There is a growing sense that AI should be used not just for the right predictions, but also to make predictions for the right reasons. While AI is getting close to humans in reading labeled data such as radiology images, the same neural network algorithms that enable machines to read images with accuracy have the potential for discriminatory profiling based on facial recognition.

The underpinnings of success with AI lie in the underlying data. Fortune 500 companies are having to set aside increasing amounts of their IT budgets for information integration today, and no sector is more acutely aware of this than healthcare, with its complex environment of proprietary EHR systems and emerging data sources. Some sectors such as consumer finance and retail are used to multi-channel engagement with customers based on an omni-data capability that can aggregate and integrate data from a wide variety of sources. Healthcare remains more siloed. Combined with an ingrained aversion to any new technology with the potential to cause harm to patients, the implications for AI adoption in healthcare are clear: It will be slower than in other sectors.

Having the data and the AI capability does not necessarily ensure improved quality or reduced costs in healthcare. Intervention models to do something with the data and care plans for preventive intervention both must be in place, which can be challenging if the data is incomplete (as is often the case with EHR data) or outdated (as with health insurance claims data). In an era of high-volume and high-velocity real-time data, these limitations will constrain the adoption of AI technologies. Other challenges include making the insights actionable and available at the point of care to drive action.

Mudit Garg, CEO and cofounder of Silicon Valley start-up Qventus, a company that combines AI with behavioral sciences to address bottlenecks in patient flow and length of stay in hospitals, has learned the hard way that AI algorithms may produce interesting insights; however, unless these insights are integrated into clinical workflows, user adoption will remain low. His company realized early on that the prediction of bottlenecks was very important, but not sufficient to drive change. In an environment where people already deal with high levels of change every day on the front lines, there is very little time for implementing new changes and also a real risk of change fatigue. Here is what Garg had to say:

> We saw that people were excited about our dashboards but did not log in to our platform when they got busy. We learned that machine-learning model predictions did not drive any action and were in fact, sometimes confusing to users. Instead, we built a platform that could process the insights and activate different actions through mobile alerts, message boards, email, or text. And that was valuable in driving action from insights.

Even with clinical workflow integration, unless there is a feedback loop, user adoption will falter, dissipating all the incremental gains. Over time, the company has worked closely with clients to develop a closed-loop system that ensures accountability for sustained outcomes for the organization.

There is an inevitability about AI's increasingly pervasive role in healthcare operations. The opportunities to make a positive impact on patient lives with AI remain significant, although the healthcare industry has been cautious about using AI in high-stakes clinical decisions. The use of AI to augment the work of administrators has gained more acceptance, especially where the risk of patient harm is relatively low and there is an abundance of data to train and validate algorithms.

Healthcare executives need to carefully consider not just whether AI is appropriate in a given situation, but also what AI techniques to use. Colt Courtright, Director of Data Analytics at Premera Blue Cross, points out,

> Nowadays, data is prolific, and the cost of collecting data from multiple sources is declining. However, data proliferation comes with new costs, especially when processing large volumes or extremely complex data sets that do not always fit neatly into columns and rows. Today's data includes X-ray images, recorded phone calls, full-motion videos, and free-flowing text messages. These new forms of data require significant investments in processing power.

Given the emphasis on predictive models for targeted communication and intervention, the choice of analytical techniques has significant implications for the overall costs of the program. While building the business case for investments in a robust analytics infrastructure and advanced analytical tools, it is important to know that more expensive solutions do not necessarily add predictive value and often result in minor incremental improvements. Healthcare enterprises should consider alternative lower cost options that are readily available today, often through third-party solutions and start-ups.

The most significant challenge with AI in healthcare is one that has been a challenge in most other industries over the past 20 years: an inherent trade-off between greater transparency and better prediction. Modern medicine has relied on traditional statistical models to provide transparency to researchers and medical practitioners. By comparison, AI in healthcare today is a black box. Because it outperforms traditional models, black box AI has become the default choice of data scientists. Classical statistics do not seem to have the interpretation value that they once did. Historically, when data was limited, predictive models were built using traditional statistics, often prescribed by a human researcher. For example, models based on classical statistics would control for interactive effects, say age and education level as a predictor of income, where age and education level are also related. Today, with prolific data and many interactive effects acting simultaneously (e.g., biological, environmental, chemical, and genetic factors), the interactive effects are complex. The correlations identified with traditional predictive models for such scenarios often lack practical value.

There are three key aspects for AI programs to be meaningful and successful, according to Steve Miff, CEO, Parkland Center for Clinical Innovation. First, AI models need to be scientifically sound and physician tested. The discipline and the rigor around the statistical analysis, modeling, and clinical input into the parameters of the models need to be sound. Second, AI cannot be a black box that generates a risk score without informing the user about the contributing reasons for the risk. The third and final aspect is to seamlessly embed AI or machine-learning models within existing workflows. Clinicians, who are hard-pressed for time, will use them if they gain access to the risk scores and recommendations from within their EHR systems.

AI will become increasingly prevalent as the volume and variety of data describing patient characteristics are taken into account, and as comparison data about patient outcomes in clinical practice versus that from controlled research studies becomes available. At the same time, the risks of increased gaps in health equity pose a real problem. Underrepresentation of certain populations in underlying data sets can distort the models and disproportionately impact certain communities.

The most popular AI approach today is deep learning, a machine-learning technique that tries to replicate the manner in which a human decodes information. The "deep" in deep learning refers to the number of layers in the decision process. There is a school of thought that deep learning does not have significantly higher predictive value over other less costly forms of AI when using traditional structured data sources (data organized in neat columns and rows). Deep learning is arguably better with unstructured and new forms of data, which is growing and is estimated to account for the majority of all healthcare data. These include images, video streams, and text. Courtright argues that unless an organization is using large data sets that are also unstructured, investment in expensive processing power is not necessary, and deep learning will not necessarily yield a better-performing predictive model. For now, though, deep learning seems to be the flavor of the month.

To appreciate some of the near-term opportunities for AI in healthcare, Courtright points to the experience of Premera Blue Cross, where he leads the advanced analytics group. Premera uses AI models to design tiered communications to their members. He says, for example, that it is possible to predict who may be considering significant procedures such as a joint replacement, making them targets for outreach and enrollment in a care management program. Today, AI models identify and predict Premera members who are likely to have an extreme escalation in healthcare needs in a given time period or be readmitted after leaving a hospital. The models can assist caregivers in prioritizing follow-up care and educating patients about self-care, all while human caregivers make the actual decisions about the right educational material or follow-up care.

In all of the cases described above, medical care itself is not determined by AI; the AI algorithm is not deciding on a diagnosis, treatment path, or medication without human intervention. The identification of health risk or a care need is where AI is adding value. Nevertheless, concerns remain about erroneous predictions (e.g., false positives or false negatives) that can be disruptive to the individual and result in additional costs.

There are three main categories of machine-learning models. One is supervised learning, where the model learns from known patterns. The majority of machine-learning models are in this category, and the method involves using labeled input data to predict outcomes. Predicting sepsis is a common application for this method. The second category is unsupervised learning, in which algorithms comb through unlabeled input data and find hidden patterns through clustering. An example of an application for unsupervised machine learning would be a patients-like-me type of analysis. Finally, in reinforcement models, the algorithms take labeled input data, interact with new data, and learn to develop a series of actions. This method is applied in chemotherapy, clinical trials, and dosing regimens, to name but a few. In applying AI to medicine, the challenge lies in applying the right model to the right situation.

Today, machine-learning models are doing well with certain data types, such as images. Google has published a widely quoted study that demonstrates how its machine-learning models were more accurate than radiologists in identifying diabetic retinopathy.* However, the practice of medicine needs more transparency and validation for AI models across a wide range of use cases. Meanwhile, nonmedical use cases are more readily accepting black box AI algorithms, and health

---

* Sayres, Rory and Krause Jonathan. "Improving the Effectiveness of Diabetic Retinopathy Models." *Google AI Blog.* December 13, 2018. Accessed December 13, 2019. https://ai.googleblog.com/2018/12/improving-effectiveness-of-diabetic.html.

systems can make use of them to remove manual tasks, automate, and deliver value rapidly.

A 2019 report by consulting firm Accenture* found that 84 percent of C-suite executives believed they must leverage artificial intelligence to achieve their growth objectives, yet 76 percent reported that they struggle to scale AI programs. The big challenges were identified as organization structure and governance (siloed and departmental initiatives), poor data quality and stewardship, and unrealistic expectations. The lack of a CEO-level focus was cited as one of the big factors impacting the scaling of AI initiatives.

Many healthcare organizations, especially the academic medical centers that we studied, are putting an enormous amount of focus on applying AI and machine learning at the highest end of the spectrum in terms of predicting mortality, curing cancer, and the like. AI clearly has the potential to help clinicians make better decisions in a number of these high-acuity areas. However, healthcare leaders must not overlook AI's utility in low-hanging fruit, which can seem very mundane but nevertheless provides useful insights that can deliver tangible benefits. An example of such an area is revenue cycle management. Healthcare leaders must also ensure that AI and machine-learning models are incorporated into the clinical workflow because that is how clinicians can really show an improvement in healthcare outcomes. Being able to predict whether a patient will have a stroke in the next 12 months and assigning a corresponding probability is certainly of value. What is even more valuable is being able to alert providers in real time based upon algorithms that can predict an adverse event by aggregating and integrating disparate clinical factors such as laboratory results and clinical documentation. As mentioned earlier, one area where machine learning has

---

* Awalegaonkar, Ketan, Robert Berkley, Greg Douglass, and Athena Reilly. "AI: Built to Scale." Accenture. November 14, 2019. Accessed December 13, 2019. www.accenture.com/us-en/insights/artificial-intelligence/ai-investments.

shown very promising results is radiology, where vast amounts of labeled images can be analyzed by machine-learning algorithms to identify nodules or early growths that aren't necessarily picked up by the human eye.

Relative to other sectors such as banking and retail, healthcare practitioners have to be cautious about applying AI to use cases where the risk of lower accuracy can have significant ramifications for patient harm. In 2019, researchers found that proprietary algorithms used by one of the leading technology firms that sells population health management tools discriminated against the sickest black patients.* Today, algorithmic bias is one of the major concerns in applying AI in a wide range of situations.

Maturing Technologies: Cloud, Voice, and Automation

Cloud

"Cloud has lowered the barriers of entry for building bigger stacks of technology platforms," says Manu Tandon, CIO at Beth Israel Deaconess Medical Center in Boston. The emergence of cloud computing is likely the most significant development in enterprise computing in the 21st century. Most CIOs that we spoke with while researching this book overwhelmingly support cloud enabling their IT and applications. Cloud service providers have undoubtedly evolved significantly over the past few years, and the benefits of cloud enablement in terms of scale, costs, and reliability are now well understood and accepted.

---

* "Population Health Tools May Exacerbate Health Disparities." Modern Healthcare. November 2, 2019. Accessed December 13, 2019. www.modernhealt hcare.com/information-technology/population-health-tools-may-exacerbate-hea lth-disparities.

As health systems architect and implement cloud solutions, it is critical that CIOs understand the impact of cloud-enabled architectures on patient care and operations. The fundamental job of an IT leader is to ensure high reliability in the IT infrastructure and high availability of applications that support the delivery of care. The design and architecture of cloud solutions will determine how well the solutions support highly reliable healthcare delivery. To ensure that the cloud solution meets expectations and also delivers a positive return on investment, IT leaders have to retain control over the orchestration of the cloud strategy and do it in a thoughtful, careful, and calculated way to deliver the best value to patients, caregivers, and the extended enterprise.

John Kravitz, CIO of Geisinger Health System, provides a straightforward assessment of the cloud choices for health systems:

> A simplistic approach is to start with a cloud-based vendor that has their own private cloud running on Amazon Web Services, Azure, or a similar platform. You have one place where you need to maintain your code and make sure it is current. EHR vendors are also migrating to the cloud because data centers are expensive.

There are other challenges as well. Finding and retaining the talent to support data center operations in an era when everything is cloud-first makes it imperative for CIOs to reconsider the traditional preferences for operating everything as an on-premises system. Besides, as Kravitz points out:

> Once you move your major EHR system to the cloud, you also have the ability to host other applications there, not just the electronic health record. I think we are therefore seeing much more migration to the cloud, and I think that is going to be a direction in which we will continue to grow.

With the exception of certain mission-critical systems, specifically EHR, most newer applications such as customer relationship management, human resources systems, IT service management, and cybersecurity are already available as cloud solutions. Even EHR systems, long seen as a bastion of on-premises deployment models, are likely to migrate to the cloud. Mayo Clinic signed a deal with Google in 2019 to migrate their primary EHR platform to the Google Cloud. The partnership also includes the Mayo Clinic Cloud Platform, which contains copies of patient medical records where Google's analytical tools will develop insights for use by Mayo Clinic in improving healthcare outcomes. Advanced analytics solutions that require hosting vast amounts of structured and unstructured data and running AI and machine-learning algorithms are increasingly located on cloud solutions such as Amazon Web Services, Microsoft Azure, or one of the other leading cloud providers. Virtually all digital health start-ups offer their solutions in cloud-based software-as-a-service models.

Daniel Barchi, Senior Vice President and CIO, New York–Presbyterian Hospital, provides some historical context:

> Ten, fifteen years ago, every health system was proud to talk about its data center and the investments it was making. Now we wonder if we really even want to own data centers. How can we get out of the data center business? Our skill set is delivering outstanding care and making people's lives better, not in running large facilities with HVAC and other fire suppression systems. I would like to put more and more of what we do into the hands of third-party companies that do it really well.

Both Barchi and Kravitz point out the downsides as well. With cloud-hosted systems, CIOs necessarily have to give up some of the flexibility of an owned and operated data center. Healthcare is generally a relatively thin-margin business on the not-for-profit side. It is relatively cheap to own a data center and keep servers there. Data centers and servers are also accounted for as capital expenditure. It is not only much more expensive to pay a third-party cloud services company such as Amazon or Microsoft to store and manage that data, but also to account for it as an operating cost year over year. As Barchi says:

> Many healthcare CIOs are dealing with complex tradeoffs while making the move to more cloud, often underestimating the fact that cloud tends to be expensive. Operationally, however, everyone recognizes there are advantages to cloud from the security, reliability, and backup point of view. But we do face the challenge of the cost.

Healthcare leaders have to think through several issues when migrating their data and mission-critical systems to the cloud. Will there be enough bandwidth? Are there contracts in place with separate Internet service providers (ISPs) that are disparate and that can provide uninterrupted service in the event we lose one ISP and lose connectivity to cloud solutions? Is it worth considering having some data reside in a local offline server in the event the entire system goes offline and all the ISPs are down? The answers to these questions become part of business continuity planning when architecting cloud-based services for health systems that expect "five nine" availability (99.999 percent uptime) or better. John M. Kravitz of Geisinger Health most likely represents the views of his peers when he says, "We will never truly get out of the data center business."

Voice Recognition and Natural Language Processing

Voice-enabled services in healthcare are only beginning to take off. The pandemic accelerated its adoption and functionality. Many health systems reported using voice to limit exposure to infected patients and reducing the amount of limited personal protection equipment required. "Voice is the most obvious next step of user interface that is going to radically change the way we interact with technology," says Dwight Raum, Chief Technology Officer at Johns Hopkins Medicine in Baltimore.

It has been estimated that the healthcare sector spends an extra billion dollars a day due to the extra time clinicians spend on documentation in their EHR systems. A study in the *Annals of Internal Medicine* estimates that since 2009, the average patient note has doubled in length to about 700 words in the United States, while patient notes in other developed countries are about a third as long. The burnout rate among clinicians, while on a declining trend, is still about 50 percent, and one study has shown that for every hour doctors spend with a clinical problem, they spend two hours on administrative work (often referred to as pajama time, since a lot of this happens after hours in their homes), a major contributor to burnout among physicians.

One emerging technology that can effectively reduce the burden of EHR documentation on clinicians is voice recognition. Early pilots have shown that using voice recognition on EHR systems can free up clinician time, increase levels of engagement and satisfaction, and reduce transcription costs. Despite error rates of around 7 percent, voice recognition will inevitably be a part of physicians' toolkit in the future for improving productivity, reducing burnout, and most importantly improving the quality of the experience for patients and caregivers alike.

"The next great natural extension of computing is ambient computing," says John Halamka, who leads the Mayo Clinic Platform initiative. Ambient computing refers to the use of voice recognition and other tools that automatically recognize and record information, eliminating the need to type into a keyboard or mobile interface. Today, systems and tools in the home have the ability to understand and interpret questions, and to even predict questions leveraging NLP and machine-learning tools. Over time, voice recognition will render most clinical systems passive interfaces for consuming and presenting clinical data, be it in an office visit, an ICU, or a clinical ward. Voice recognition will provide clinicians with the ability to focus on delivering care, untethered by the keyboard, which has been the bane of clinician workflows and a big contributor to unsatisfactory patient experiences, medical errors, and burnout since the advent of EHRs and the digitization of patient medical records.

"I envision a day 20 years from now when a CIO will be talking about the day when keyboards disappeared," says David Quirke, CIO of Inova Health System. His prediction may come true much sooner than that. In late 2019, Amazon launched a speech-recognition tool that enables clinicians to dictate clinical notes and to accurately convert those notes into text that feeds directly into EHR systems. Using an inconspicuous array of microphones in patient rooms, Rush University Medical Center and the University of Nebraska Medical Center, in collaboration with technology provider Nuance Communications, have developed an ambient clinical intelligence system that combines conversational AI, speech synthesis, and NLP to record and respond to physicians in real time. The system has the potential to dramatically increase physician productivity, reduce burnout, and save costs, while improving the quality of care. Nuance has forged a partnership with Microsoft to use ambient technology, artificial intelligence, automation, and cloud computing to create an exam room experience where the clinical documentation writes itself.

Following the waves of web and mobile, voice recognition has potentially been the next major influence in the user interface and technology platform shift of the past two decades. Indeed, voice recognition may be the next battleground for big tech firms as consumers increasingly use voice interfaces to access information, much like how Google's search engine dominated consumer attention for years. Amazon made news when details of its proposed emotion-sensing wearable device came to light in early 2019. Studies have established the use of voice recognition to detect early stages of Parkinson's disease, and we can expect the same technologies to be used to detect and treat a range of conditions. Amazon, with reportedly over 10,000 associates on its Alexa team, is not alone in turning voice-recognition technology toward solving healthcare problems. Besides Amazon, Google (Google Assistant), Apple (Siri), and Microsoft (Cortana) are also investing billions of dollars to gain a dominant position in the voice-based personal assistant market (or at least not be left behind).

Voice recognition is going to play an important role in the future of healthcare delivery and the way health systems interact with technology. Consumers increasingly want their healthcare delivered at a time, place, and manner of their choosing. If AI algorithms have their way, in some cases, the time of delivery might be before consumers even realize they need care. North-Carolina–based Atrium Health's Alexa pilot is using voice recognition to help customers identify a nearby urgent care center and get a same-day appointment. This will significantly improve access and drive consumer satisfaction, not to mention the bottom-line impact from increased revenues for the health system. There have been ample studies about how the advent of EHR systems and technology in general has increased the workload for physicians and other caregivers. The next wave of technologies is expected to reduce the burden of caregivers, and voice recognition fits neatly into that picture.

Delivering superior experiences is one of the primary goals of any digital transformation. As we enter the era of zero-user-interface technology, where a touchscreen is replaced by a natural language interface such as voice recognition, technology starts to dissolve into the background of our everyday experience. The capabilities that voice recognition enables, such as those in the Alexa pilot described earlier, will achieve that in the near term for a range of simple tasks. However, over time the software will significantly improve more complex customer experiences. As the voice-recognition software becomes more sophisticated, with the help of AI and machine learning, it will adjust to accents and a broader range of terminologies. The latter aspect becomes critical in a medical context as clinical terminology is progressively built into the lexicon of the interface.

However, consumer-grade voice-recognition services, such as asking for a restaurant recommendation, do not always translate to healthcare technology. Healthcare is bound by HIPAA data privacy rules that govern what information can be shared, with whom, and how. Amazon has released a set of Alexa skills that transmit and receive protected health information pertaining to relatively mundane services, such as status updates for prescription refills; however, these pilot projects set up a testbed for secure communication for a range of complex care management protocols down the road.

As healthcare increasingly shifts to tending and caring for people in a home setting, tools and technologies around understanding voice will be important enablers for virtual care models. Voice-recognition software understands words and infers context. The software can extract diagnosis, problem lists, and prescription lists with a high degree of confidence from unstructured data, turning it into structured data, which can in turn be fed into machine-learning models. In the future, voice recognition will thus no longer just be a recording tool, but will become part of the diagnostic process in clinical decision support, enhancing not just clinical productivity, but the quality of the patient experience and ultimately the quality of healthcare outcomes.

Voice recognition is already a part of consumers' lives for a variety of other services, such as banking and retail. If there is a roadblock to increasing the use of voice-enabled services in healthcare, it would be concerns around privacy, especially if the data from voice-based interactions are stored in a cloud by one of the big tech firms. Reports of Amazon's Alexa snooping on consumers generate the kind of concerns that hinder efforts to expand the technology until sufficient privacy safeguards are established. Over time, these concerns will be addressed, much as concern about patient data storage in cloud infrastructure is no longer an issue today.

In early 2019, Providence Health in Washington launched Grace, a *chatbot* whose job description is symptom triage. Grace enables healthcare consumers to describe their symptoms on a mobile device. Using a triaging algorithm, Grace helps consumers decide on an action (e.g., whether to schedule a clinic visit). Aaron Martin, Chief Digital Officer of Providence Health, says, "You're going to see chatbots become pervasive and contextually aware over time. As we simplify the health system, chatbots like Grace will navigate you through the complexity of the healthcare experience all along the way." This early investment paid off. Grace allowed Providence Health to respond quickly to the pandemic. Over time, chatbots will become important enablers of remote care models as they interface with technologies that are already in the home, such as Google's Nest or Amazon's HIPAA-enabled Alexa. Physicians in clinics can already use bots as virtual scribes. Chatbots will eventually evolve to take on more intelligent tasks such as order entry, allowing physicians to simply verify and submit the final entries into the EHR system.

A related technology that has made a significant impact in replacing labor in operational areas is robotic process automation (RPA). Using intelligent automation, RPA tools can learn and repeat routine tasks performed by humans in a variety of functional areas. In healthcare, notable examples have demonstrated benefits in back-office processes such as revenue cycle management and claims processing operations. Daniel Barchi from New York–Presbyterian Hospital has redeployed hundreds of talented people on his finance teams who did repetitive tasks to value-added activities such as solving complex problems for the health system and for their patients. Barchi is expanding his fleet of bots to increase back-office efficiencies so that he and his teams can be more customer focused.

We see the increasing use of bots all across healthcare and in other industries as well. Over time, high-value use cases involving bots could include front-office functions, such as helping clinicians to prioritize and work their patient queues and for routing to specialists, or simply for mundane activities such as reminders and rescheduling of appointments that lighten up workloads. RPA has significant promise for cost savings as well as lessening burdens on clinicians. The impact on the healthcare workforce from the extensive use of intelligent automation tools could be the elimination of certain jobs altogether, which has been a concern across industry sectors.

Emerging Technologies: 5G, Blockchain

Digital health innovation relies on many aspects of the underlying infrastructure. Network reliability is an important one. With healthcare shifting from the hospital to the home, IoT devices such as wearables and sensors are playing an increasingly important role in care delivery. There are also more medical services being performed from mobile clinics and ambulances. All of these modalities of care delivery require a new generation of network architecture for reliability and responsiveness.

In early 2019, Rush University Medical Center in Chicago made news when it announced that it would become the first hospital to build a standards-based 5G network in a healthcare setting. 5G is an emerging technology that is being touted for its transformative potential in enabling everything from super-fast movie downloads to performing robotic surgery from across the world. However, much of what 5G claims to accomplish can be done today through regular wireless networks, at least in most healthcare settings. Implementing 5G on a large scale is going to require blanketing vast areas with short-range antennas, which can be logistically challenging in dense urban areas as well in older buildings with thick walls – a situation that many leading hospitals across the country face today. For now, in the context of healthcare, 5G may simply be a technology solution looking for a problem.

Blockchain is an emerging technology that came into the limelight when bitcoin, a form of digital currency, emerged as a new form of payment a few years ago. In simple terms, blockchain technology enables an immutable record of transactions maintained in a distributed digital ledger online across multiple networked devices and cannot be modified or deleted. A 2017 study on blockchain adoption in healthcare by Black Book Market Research indicated that a large percentage of healthcare payers and a small but growing percentage of providers were either considering deploying or were in the process of implementing some blockchain solution sets. Some technology solution providers, including IBM, Change Healthcare, and a number of other companies listed in the Black Book study, have made significant moves in establishing blockchain capabilities and launching solutions. Federal agencies such as the Food and Drug Administration and Centers for Disease Control and Prevention have expressed interest in applying blockchain technology to find solutions for public health issues.

However, despite the promise, blockchain technology has made limited progress in healthcare. There continues to be considerable confusion about what blockchain technology is and does. The most promising use cases seem to pertain to ensuring data integrity across multiple systems and settings, using blockchain ledgers that also serve as immutable records of transactions. One of the significant initiatives related to blockchain technology in healthcare has been the formation of the Synaptic Health Alliance, a consortium of large healthcare enterprises tasked with solving one of the most significant data challenges in healthcare today: provider data management. Provider data, a fundamental enabler of healthcare transactions, is a key building block for processing claims and maintaining up-to-date provider directories. Today, most provider data are stored in siloed and independent databases. Provider data quality is estimated to be a $2.1-billion problem today, according to a report by CAQH, a nonprofit alliance focused on creating shared initiatives to streamline the business of healthcare. By streamlining the inefficiencies in provider data maintenance, participants can have a single source of truth and significantly reduce provider data management costs using blockchain solutions.

Tech firms such as IBM have been active in promoting blockchain use cases. Amazon, with its closely watched entry into healthcare, has also announced the launch of blockchain templates for healthcare, aimed at making it easier for developers to create blockchain-based projects and deploy blockchain networks via open-source frameworks. The initial mania around bitcoin, the very first use case for blockchain, is now giving way to more carefully considered use cases for business with tangible benefits. Healthcare, a sector that generally lags behind in the adoption of technologies, is currently in a wait-and-watch mode. As with most transformative technologies, the big challenge is not the technology; it is managing culture and changes to workflow and processes. Blockchain technology necessitates a commitment and willingness to work across company boundaries, which is an entirely new paradigm for most healthcare enterprises.

The potential for blockchain technology to improve healthcare operating efficiencies is significant. High-value use cases include revenue cycle management, supply chain, clinical trials, and provider data management. The initial pilots will need to demonstrate the real benefits of the technology and lead to higher adoption of blockchain in the coming years. Our best hope is that the early pilots will bring tangible proof of its benefits and provide more confidence to the industry.

Key Takeaways and Action Steps

1. Modern and emerging technologies are essential components of the digital transformation toolkit. There are unprecedented choices of technology platforms to enable the digital health experience of the future. Carefully assess those at your disposal and deploy them alongside your legacy technologies to drive patient and caregiver experiences.

2. In an era of data-driven decision-making, machine learning and AI tools can provide valuable insights to transform healthcare experiences. These tools have demonstrated benefits in a range of administrative functions but are in early stages for clinical decisions. Focus on areas where you can demonstrate short-term wins and build an organizational culture that accepts AI-enabled decision-making to drive efficiencies and improved healthcare delivery outcomes.

3. The rapid growth of cloud computing and the rise of cloud-only software-as-a-service solutions require healthcare organizations to develop enterprise cloud strategies to support digital transformation. Cloud is not an answer to everything, yet. Assess your cloud-enablement opportunities and understand the trade-offs between operating costs and incremental efficiencies. Work closely with your technology partners to manage cloud migrations.

4. Voice-recognition technology is maturing rapidly and is expected to progressively replace keyboard-based interfaces. Evaluate the potential of voice-enabled interfaces and AI to develop ambient computing environments and reduce the burden on physician workloads.

5. Carefully monitor the progress of emerging technologies in healthcare applications. Position yourself to be on the leading edge, not the bleeding edge.

6. Question new investments in on-premises applications and consider a cloud migration roadmap for existing applications.
7. Retreat idea: Convene a series of workshops to develop high-level roadmaps for the following: cloud migration of enterprise workloads, voice enablement of patient and caregiver experiences, and AI enablement in clinical use cases.

30-SECOND AGILE CONSULT

What will be the most disruptive technology in healthcare in the next five years and why? How has pandemic experience changed this or did it?

Chapter 6

Building Technology Partnerships for Success

Healthcare's digital transformation is critically dependent on strategic partnerships with technology vendors. The technology vendor landscape is undergoing its own transformation as it restructures itself to meet the needs of healthcare organizations in the digital era. In the short term, many technology vendors are leading with marketing messages that proclaim their digital capabilities. Healthcare leaders must review their current relationships with incumbent vendors to assess their suitability for future needs while evaluating the capabilities of the emerging class of digital health innovators to reimagine their patient and caregiver experiences. They must recognize that there is no single vendor that can meet all the needs of digital transformation. Organizations will need to develop their digital platform partnerships with vendors based on a structured evaluation of their business models and attributes. The ICEA™ framework described in this chapter guides the understanding of the technology vendor landscape to develop a partnership strategy for a digital future.

Understanding the Technology Vendor Ecosystem: ICEA™ Framework

Healthcare is not a winner-take-all industry. Unlike in highly concentrated segments such as search advertising or social media that are dominated by a small number of firms that effectively shut out any new competition, there is ample room for emerging tech firms and innovators in the digital health landscape. In the past few years, as several industry sectors have scrambled to reimagine their businesses for a digital era, incumbent technology vendors and a new breed of digital health start-ups have set out to capitalize on the opportunity. Many technology firms have successfully done so or are well on their way. As an example, cloud computing is all but mainstream today, a far cry from the skepticism around cloud enablement just a few years ago. Voice-recognition technologies, natural language interfaces, and artificial intelligence (AI) have made remarkable progress in care delivery innovation. However, just like their enterprise customers, technology vendors face significant challenges in making the transition to the future.

The technology leaders of previous decades are now under threat of being disrupted. Consider these examples. GE Healthcare, after several attempts to muscle its way into the electronic health record (EHR) business and spending hundreds of millions of dollars on building a digital business around its Predix platform for the industrial Internet, is now in an existential crisis.* IBM's Watson Health business, launched with high expectations following the spectacular performance of the Watson cognitive computing engine on the TV show *Jeopardy!* in 2012, has failed to live up to its promise, suffering

---

* Gryta, Thomas and Ted Mann. *GE Powered the American Century – Then It Burned Out*. December 14, 2018. Accessed January 28, 2020. www.wsj.com/art icles/ge-powered-the-american-centurythen-it-burned-out-11544796010.

a series of negative media reports* about missed expectations and at least one high-profile separation with the MD Anderson Cancer Center.† Contrast the GE and IBM stories with that of Microsoft, a company that, under CEO Satya Nadella, has dramatically increased shareholder value over a five-year period to become one of the first-ever companies to reach a trillion dollars in market capitalization.‡ Microsoft, along with other tech giants, notably Amazon, Apple, and Google, is aggressively pursuing dominance in the healthcare market. Among the dominant EHR vendors, publicly held Cerner and Allscripts have made acquisitions an essential aspect of their market strategy, while privately held Epic has committed itself to organic growth. The collective challenge for all technology vendors is to maintain relevance in the emerging digital health era.

An emerging crop of digital health companies, fueled by billions in venture capital (VC), are trying to remake healthcare delivery with a technology-led approach. What the new breed of companies enjoys is the freedom to pursue their business models without the burden of technical debt that many of the larger tech firms have to contend with. However, Daniel Barchi of New York–Presbyterian Hospital also believes that start-ups are generally years away from being well integrated into the core EHR systems. While none of the new breed of digital health companies has reached "unicorn" status (over a billion dollars in valuation or market capitalization), some surely will in the future, disrupting many established

---

* Ross, Casey. *How an IBM Watson Health Rescue Mission Collapsed – And a Top Executive Was Ousted.* November 1, 2018. Accessed January 29, 2020. www.s tatnews.com/2018/11/01/ibm-watson-health-natural-language-processing/.

† Herper, Matthew. *MD Anderson Benches IBM Watson in Setback for Artificial Intelligence in Medicine.* February 19, 2017. Accessed January 29, 2020. www.f orbes.com/sites/matthewherper/2017/02/19/md-anderson-benches-ibm-watso n-in-setback-for-artificial-intelligence-in-medicine/#545467b43774.

‡ Weise, Karen. *Microsoft's Profit Rises 19% as Its Cloud Business Drives Strong Results.* April 24, 2019. Accessed January 29, 2020. www.nytimes.com/2019/04/24 /technology/microsoft-earnings.html.

technology firms in the process. A slew of successful digital health initial public offerings in 2019* provide us with confidence and hope about what lies ahead.

VC-funded start-ups are not the only ones innovating. Big tech firms are innovating as well, as are many leading health systems that have successfully managed to assemble cross-functional groups comprising clinicians and technologists to bring innovative ideas to life and even commercialize them through spin-offs. In the book *Voices of Innovation*† (edited by Ed), there are several vignettes describing how leading health systems are creating cross-functional teams of clinicians, technologists, and operations experts to develop innovations every day to transform care delivery.

Understanding the market structure and attributes of different types of technology vendors is important for healthcare executives developing digital transformation roadmaps. Healthcare organizations, as we have pointed out earlier, have a very limited margin for error, and choosing the wrong vendor can significantly derail digital transformation efforts. Vendors, for their part, must appreciate that health systems are risk-averse and fast followers at best, and for good reason. Vendors have to recognize the core business drivers and the changing competitive landscape of healthcare organizations and reimagine their own businesses to align with new marketplace needs, which are often unclear to the market participants themselves. Many technology firms must acknowledge that the skills and product capabilities that made them successful in a prior era of healthcare may not be enough to maintain relevance in the future. Technology vendors must go beyond

---

* Day, Sean and Elena Gambon. 2019. *In 2019, Digital Health Celebrated Six IPOs as Venture Investment Edged Off Record Highs.* Accessed January 27, 2020. https://rockhealth.com/reports/in-2019-digital-health-celebrated-six-ipos-as-venture-investment-edged-off-record-highs/?mc_cid=2e313c0fee&mc_eid=92f95b707d.
† Marx, Edward W. *Voices of Innovation: Fulfilling the Promise of Information Technology in Healthcare (HIMSS Book Series).* Orlando: CRC Press, 2019. https://books.google.co.in/books?id=9vSDDwAAQBAJ&hl=en.

relabeling their traditional offerings as digital; they must reinvent themselves, just as their customers are. Customers expect digital health innovators to recognize the real problems clinicians face in delivery care and work backward to develop a solution. Technology vendors, especially start-ups, must also resist the temptation to overbuild solutions and instead co-develop/co-innovate in close collaboration with their customers, validating the solution every step of the way.

Healthcare organizations have traditionally preferred off-the-shelf solutions to custom-developed solutions. The role of traditional IT services firms has been limited in light of this dynamic. However, as consumer preferences start to drive unique and specialized experiences, and as the need to manage multiple data sources, integration points, and modalities of care grows, healthcare organizations will need specialized capabilities that can be provided by global technology firms with broad and deep technical talent pools. In the face of talent shortages, healthcare organizations will also need to repurpose their pool of internal resources to future-state technologies and outsource the management of legacy technologies.

While some may think that healthcare organizations are going to be disrupted by big technology firms with vast resources at their disposal, Dr. Toby Cosgrove of Cleveland Clinic disagrees: "I think the idea that there's going to be a major disruption in healthcare is difficult to imagine." Big tech's success with healthcare is not foretold in any way. Both Google and Microsoft have failed previously in consumer health. However, the big tech firms can continue to invest indefinitely in healthcare because of the vast financial resources at their disposal. Indeed, all the major tech firms have declared their intent to stay invested in healthcare for the long term.

In the book *The Big Unlock* (authored by Paddy), the four major categories of technology providers are identified as Innovators, Custodians, Enablers, and Arbitrageurs.

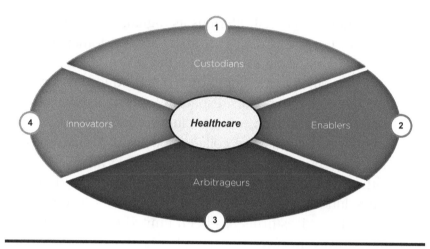

Figure 6.1   Technology vendors: ICEA™ framework. Source: Padmanabhan 2017*

These categories are represented in the ICEA™ framework in Figure 6.1. We start with the Innovators because this category of solution providers is redefining the health care experience more than any other category in our framework. Innovators are not only finding solutions to problems that are yet to be addressed but doing it in an entirely new way compared to traditional technology firms, using agile approaches and human-centered design principles. Most importantly, many innovators come from outside the healthcare sector and bring a fresh perspective to the problems of healthcare.

Innovators: We Have a Whole New Way of Doing It

Innovators are digital health start-ups that are looking to redefine care delivery by designing engaging user experiences leveraging data and analytics in a mobile-first, cloud-first

* Padmanabhan, Paddy. *THE BIG UNLOCK – Harnessing Data and Growing Digital Health Businesses in a Value-Based Care Era.* 2017. Chicago, IL: Archway Publishing.

approach. Innovators are nimble, responsive, and flexible. However, they tend to be small firms that are heavily reliant on a few key individuals and are constantly under financial pressure. They also tend to be unfamiliar with the long sales cycles of healthcare enterprises. The success of many high-profile digital health initial public offerings in 2019 signaled that a sizable cohort of *Innovators* is coming of age, although nearly $30 billion remains locked up in illiquid digital health investments.* While many start-ups are focused on developing last-mile solutions to address critical gaps or improvement areas in care delivery in the digital health space (digital health start-ups raised $7.4 billion in capital in 2019[†]), there is a shortage of *viable and proven* digital health solutions for health systems and their key stakeholders in healthcare delivery (i.e., patients and caregivers), which we refer to as the last-mile problem.

Enabler platforms are designed to enable the developer community and end customers to build the last-mile solutions that Innovators are focused on building. Digital leaders in healthcare organizations have to carefully assess Enabler platforms in terms of the additional efforts and costs of deployment, the technical risks, and the trade-offs between custom development and off-the-shelf purchases. A common feature among start-ups is that they offer their solutions almost entirely in a software-as-a-service (SaaS) model, leveraging the infrastructure-as-a-service models of the major cloud providers as a backbone for their applications.

Healthcare technology leaders also have to be watchful of the widespread practice by technology firms in general to overstate the capabilities of their solutions in an effort to

---

* Day, Sean. "2019 Midyear Digital Health Market Update: Exits Are Heating Up." Rock Health. Accessed December 13, 2019. https://rockhealth.com/reports/2019-midyear-digital-health-market-update-exits-are-heating-up/.
[†] Lovett, Laura. *Digital Health Funding Deals Dipped in 2019 to $7.4B, per Rock Health.* January 08, 2020. Accessed January 29, 2020. www.mobihealthnews.com/news/digital-health-funding-deals-dipped-2019-74b-rock-health.

gain traction. While there are hundreds of start-ups catering to a wide range of healthcare consumer and caregiver needs, relatively few of them have gone on to become successful companies. After a string of failed experiments in the direct-to-consumer market, many digital health companies pivoted to a B2B model and have learned to overcome the unique challenges inherent in healthcare, such as regulation and long sales cycles. Leah Sparks, CEO and Co-founder of Wildflower Health, a digital health company that supports women during their pregnancies, says, "A theme that we see in digital transformation is that it often has to start with simple use cases and grow from there." While firms like Wildflower Health have seen growth and adoption, the path to success for many promising and innovative start-ups is marked by significant roadblocks. "The risks are high in healthcare," says Sparks. "It's hard for healthcare to experiment on things that don't have an obvious return on investment."

The most dreaded roadblock for digital health start-ups today is "death by pilot." The effort, costs, and risks of bringing a viable product into the market are so high that many start-ups burn through available capital and go out of business while waiting for health systems to accelerate the adoption of their solutions. Others try to cut corners, following the credo of "fake it till you make it." Highly public failures such as Theranos, a blood testing start-up that rose to prominence rapidly and fell just as quickly when reports of questionable business practices and the lack of a real business model emerged,* stand witness to the perils of shortcuts. There are other risks too, such as governance, when it comes to start-ups. One Silicon Valley start-up that we visited had developed what looked like a very interesting digital health platform and had raised tens of millions of dollars from name-brand VCs.

---

* Carreyrou, John. *Blood-Testing Firm Theranos to Dissolve.* September 5, 2018. Accessed January 28, 2020. www.wsj.com/articles/blood-testing-firm-theranos-to-dissolve-1536115130.

A few months after our visit, the company's board of directors ousted its founder/CEO and the company has since pretty
much dropped out of sight, possibly taking millions in VC
money down with them.

Drew Schiller, Founder and CEO of digital health start-up
Validic, has an alternative explanation for the failure of many
digital health start-ups:

> I think a lot of digital health companies have built their
> solutions to deliver clinical value. But the problem is that
> those solutions do not necessarily deliver financial value.
> The truth of the matter is that, in this day and age, health
> systems especially, but even commercial health plans,
> really need to see that a dollar invested in a solution with
> a vendor is going to yield more than that dollar back.
> Ideally, two or three dollars back in indirect revenue.

From the viewpoint of healthcare consumers, digital health solutions have to connect to their healthcare through a channel and
brand that they trust, and they don't necessarily trust the many
consumer health brands in the market. However, if their clinician, doctor, or even their health plan recommends a technology
solution and makes it available under their brands, consumers
are more likely to trust it. Xealth, a company incubated within
Providence Ventures (the venture arm of Providence Health),
has tried to address this challenge by developing a platform that
curates digital health start-ups and removes the friction involved
in managing them, such as integration, ease of use, and contract management. Mike McSherry, CEO of Xealth, believes that
digital health solutions have to be doctor prescribed and refers
to the platform as a "digital health formulary"* that aims to make

---

* McSherry, Mike and Paddy Padmanabhan. "Episode 17: Digital Health Solutions
Should Be 'Doctor Prescribed.'" Podcast Audio. *The Big Unlock Podcast.*
Accessed December 13, 2019. https://thebigunlock.com/the-big-unlock-podcast-e
pisode-17/.

services available on the platform with a single click on a doctor's EHR user interface.

One of the biggest challenges for start-ups is getting organization-wide buy-in from their clients. "If you don't have broad organizational buy-in, it's very, very hard to scale something," says Graham Gardner, MD, CEO, and Founder of Kyruus. Gardner has a counterintuitive suggestion to address this challenge: "What we've noticed over the years is that as our deal size has gotten larger, it commands more attention from the organization, and those end up being much more successful implementations." While broad enterprise buy-in provides a way out of pilot purgatory, the downside to this approach is that larger deal sizes can lengthen deal cycles even further. Many tech start-ups are also susceptible to a particular fallacy when it comes to healthcare: While every digital health start-up aims to build technology solutions that will have a significant and far-reaching impact on cost and quality for health systems, the reality is that not every problem can be solved with technology. Indeed, throwing technology at the wrong problem may increase the costs of care due to additional interventions that may result from ineffective use. "We can't just come in and think we can solve things from a tech perspective," says Gardner.

The reality is that healthcare is different, and there is not a lot of margin for error with technology solutions in most healthcare organizations. "We don't want to invest in shiny things that don't help our health system move forward," says Sylvia Romm, Chief Innovation Officer at Atlantic Health System in New Jersey. Romm believes that a patient-centered focus is vital to healthcare innovation, and she works with Atlantic Health System's team members and physicians to find new ways to improve access to high-quality and affordable care. Her previous experience with a leading video-based telemedicine company has sensitized her to the importance of ensuring broad-based support across stakeholder groups for the success of any digital health innovation program.

Despite the many failures, there are also several start-up successes, and new business models are reimagining the healthcare experience from the ground up. However, a big challenge that health systems face is the lack of resources or willingness to work with a large number of small companies directly. For many start-ups, digital health comes down to just an app. Start-ups that develop interesting technology also get stuck trying to figure out a healthcare problem to apply it to, essentially attacking the issue backward. Greg Silvesti,* Head of Digital Innovation at AbbVie, makers of blockbuster drug Humira, suggests many start-ups are too enamored by the "widget." He urges companies to focus more on the problems that enterprises are trying to solve, for example, in a patient population, and then working toward the ultimate solution for that patient population.

Lately, health systems have acknowledged that they need to do more to enable successful start-ups by developing clear pathways and milestones for innovative solutions to scale to enterprise-wide adoption. Chief innovation officers in health systems are aligning themselves to the strategic priorities of the enterprise and focusing their efforts on identifying and integrating innovative solutions to help achieve enterprise goals. Often their roles overlap with the positions of chief information officers and chief digital officers. Our research† indicates that the innovation function in healthcare is often combined with other roles, such as chief digital officer or chief technology officer. Regardless of where the innovation function sits, there is clearly a need for active collaboration between individuals with responsibilities for the IT, digital, and

---

* Padmanabhan, Paddy. "Price of Entry or Corporate Strategy: How Pharma and Biotech Are Approaching Digital Health." CIO. January 10, 2019. Accessed December 13, 2019. www.cio.com/article/3332681/price-of-entry-or-corporate-strategy-how-pharma-and-biotech-are-approaching-digital-health.html.

† "The Current State of Healthcare Digital Transformation." Damo Consulting. Accessed December 13, 2019. www.damoconsulting.net/2019/07/30/the-current-state-of-healthcare-digital-transformation/.

innovation functions. At some point, some of these roles may merge or even go away (remember chief data officer?).

Manu Tandon, CIO of Beth Israel Deaconess Medical Center, says:

> Paying attention to workflow is not enough to have a smart solution. It has to be put in the context of a very fast-paced work pattern. The opportunity to impact lives is a short window where you can impact the decision making of a physician. My advice to start-ups is that the less data you need for your solution, the better.

Tandon suggests that creating new technically smart solutions is not the only way to disrupt healthcare; the process and the people side of it are just as important.

Health systems need innovation. The choice to partner with innovative start-ups is exciting but risky. Leveraging the start-up ecosystem can limit a health system's ability to scale due to the investment and effort in nurturing each solution, not to mention having to deal with contracting and vendor management for a large number of small entities that can consume a disproportionate amount of resources. To complicate matters, many digital health start-ups fail to invest adequately in compliance, data privacy, and security in their thirst for growth, increasing the risks even further for health systems that utilize the tools. Recognizing this challenge, some of the major tech firms have been growing their ecosystem of partnerships by encouraging start-ups to build on their platforms and often certifying such partners to provide assurance to healthcare enterprises looking to tap into the innovation. EHR vendor Epic does exactly that for digital health partners on their App Orchard* store, providing a degree of assurance for the numerous solutions offered on the store and acting as a perceived

---

* "App Orchard." *Epic*. Accessed December 13, 2019. https://apporchard.epic.com/.

risk-mitigator by health systems. When it comes to big tech firms and their health clouds, this approach comes with the caveat that health systems either already have or will need to make a strategic commitment to one or more of the major tech platforms to tap into the innovation. Another option for health systems is to selectively enter into risk-sharing agreements with digital health start-ups and gradually ease into a conventional payment model as required. However, risk-sharing models not only are hard to implement but may also result in the health system giving away more of the gains from the deployment of the technology than they may be comfortable with.

The challenge for health systems, as well as the digital health innovators that serve them, remains one of alignment in financial interest. Health systems are pursuing innovation today as stand-alone projects, mostly around patient engagement and telehealth. In the absence of an enterprise-level digital transformation strategy, many innovation initiatives remain suboptimal in their impact. When asked about how start-ups should be approaching the markets, Mike McSherry of Xealth says, "Know who's paying for the solution. Follow the money, which is an often-repeated thread when jumping into healthcare. Be humble and listen to your audiences." Providers will often speak up about a problem with their care delivery that provides an opportunity to build a solution. Start-ups can significantly increase their chances of success by working with providers to develop new care pathways using innovative technology and capability.

The stakes for healthcare organizations are very high when it comes to patient safety and care delivery, and because of this, many healthcare organizations are averse to the risks of introducing new technology to patients and clinicians. Moreover, many of them are very large institutions, where decision-making is slow, and sometimes appear to be needlessly bureaucratic. The singular challenge for digital health innovators, except for the few trying to reach consumers directly, is to reconcile with the uniqueness of healthcare and the slow pace of technology adoption relative to other sectors. Leah Sparks of Wildflower Health is optimistic. She says:

> I do think that healthcare systems and plans have become more willing to take a leap of faith than they were earlier. They feel the pressure even more than they did seven years ago to embrace digital, especially great digital experiences for the patient.

The digital transformation of healthcare is in its early stages, and the gold rush is underway. Despite the remarkable response to the COVID-19 pandemic in the form of digital front doors and telehealth applications that virtualize the experience of healthcare, the digital health landscape suffers from a highly fragmented ecosystem of point solutions with few real solutions to deploy with speed and scale and a surfeit of big technology firms looking to make long-term multi-million dollar commitments for enabling platforms.

The problem that tech firms and start-ups run into in healthcare is that it is seen as the land of opportunity because of the size of the sector and the obvious inefficiencies begging for new solutions. Given that healthcare is a low-margin business with known preferences for investments with quick returns, there is also a tendency for start-ups and innovators to focus on smaller problems where a solution can quickly demonstrate a positive return on investment. The paradox is that the solutions often fail to get traction within the health system or insurer because it is not top of mind at the CEO level. Another common mistake is that start-ups, especially those that receive large funding rounds from VCs, tend to overbuild the company and the solution. The mindset is one that arises from operating in winner-take-all markets, where opportunities are often considered perishable if a company does not gain a high market share relatively quickly. Companies that overbuild from a product standpoint as well as from a sales force standpoint often burn through available cash as they grapple with the long sales cycles of 12–18 months that are common in healthcare.

Aaron Martin, Chief Digital Officer of Providence Health, has some valuable advice for digital health start-ups:

> You have got to have a small story and a big story. The small story is how you are going to deliver value in the next 6–18 months to whoever you are selling to. If you do not have that nailed down to a financial payback, you are not going to get anywhere at scale. The big story is for the VCs and chief digital officers and is about where the whole idea is going. If you solve a problem with the small story, and the big story convinced me that this isn't just an interesting point solution but one that becomes a bigger solution over time, then you've earned the right to build out the business based on your success with the small story. And then you have to make sure the problem you're working on is one of the top 10 on a health system's agenda.

So far, one thing is clear: No single tech firm seems positioned to dominate healthcare in the short term. While the major EHR vendors have established a strong footprint with high switching costs among health systems across the country, the market seems to have plenty of room for emerging companies – incumbents, innovators, or start-ups – to carve out a role in the digital transformation of healthcare. For all these reasons, platforms are only just gaining significance, and it may be early days yet; however, we are beginning to see several success stories that could define the digital future of healthcare.

Each of the categories of technology providers in this chapter has its unique strengths. While it does not seem likely that a dominant digital health platform will emerge in the near term, the window of opportunity for innovators is narrowing. As the high-value white spaces get filled up and the risks of failure increase, VCs are committing larger and larger amounts of funding to more mature companies in the hope of a successful exit. New entrants in the innovation landscape will need to either find new white spaces or build better mousetraps to challenge well-capitalized incumbents on their turf. At the same time, as the pace of exits picks up, VC firms will look for new investment opportunities for their liquidation gains. For now, it is best for digital health innovators to operate with an abundance mindset.

Custodians: We Have the Data and the Workflow

Custodians are mainly the big EHR vendors that have custody of the data and enable the workflow in health systems. Ideally, any healthcare organization will work with just one EHR vendor. For the purpose of this book, we will ignore transaction systems for back-office functions such as HR and finance, which are also Custodian platforms. One way to describe EHR platforms is to see them as the scaffolding for building the digital infrastructure for healthcare delivery in the future and as the robust technology foundation on which digital health innovations can be developed. The reality is that health systems are spending a significant amount of time and resources optimizing their EHR systems on an ongoing basis. At their extreme, EHR systems can be a distraction that continues to consume scarce resources, limiting the organization's ability to accelerate the pace of digital transformation. As systems of record, EHR vendors enjoy the long-term strategic commitment of the health systems they serve and are the first port-of-call whenever a health system decides to enable new functionality to enhance the patient and caregiver experience.

Custodians are usually deeply entrenched in enterprises (think of enterprise resource planning systems in other industries). Daniel Barchi, CIO of New York–Presbyterian, speaks for many health system CIOs when he acknowledges the primary role of EHR systems in healthcare IT:

> We are really focused on our core electronic medical record. And let us be honest, that is where our clinicians spend the bulk of their day. We want everything to be accessible through the electronic medical record. We don't want [doctors to have to] do core data, documentation, and ordering in the electronic medical record, but when they want to use a cool decision support tool, log out of the EMR and log into this other system.

EHR vendors have deep knowledge of clinical workflows and wide and deep enterprise relationships. The platforms are mostly deployed as on-premises software today as opposed to the cloud-first model of emerging technology solutions. Their usefulness as highly reliable systems for capturing clinical transactions for billing purposes has overshadowed their limitations, such as poor user experience design or the lack of advanced analytics capabilities, which are critical for a digitally reimagined healthcare experience. Health systems have made huge investments – tens and hundreds of millions of dollars – in platforms such as Epic and Cerner, which makes switching costs extremely prohibitive.

The rapid consolidation among health systems poses a challenge to CIOs: Should they consolidate the EHR systems as well, for which there is a limited business justification? The question for other big tech firms and innovators is how to build digital solutions that interface seamlessly with EHR platforms. A contentious issue in this regard has been the ongoing challenge with data interoperability; however, with the emergence of API-led connectivity to leverage data exposed through HL7 and FHIR standards, there is a significant reduction in the friction involved in getting disparate health systems to talk to one another. Big tech firms such as Microsoft, Amazon, Apple, and Google are actively collaborating with the major EHR vendors to facilitate data exchange and cloud enablement, while creating new and engaging digital experiences driven by real-time insights from advanced analytics and machine-learning tools.

Notwithstanding the strong pushback from the physician community to the poor user interfaces and additional data entry work (described in colorful detail by Dr. Atul Gawande in his *New Yorker* piece titled "Why Doctors Hate Their Computers"),* hospital administrators and CIOs continue to look to their primary EHR vendors as the default option for advanced analytics and digital health experiences.

In one major health system, Cleveland Clinic, the digital transformation leader worked with cross-functional stakeholders and mapped the list of digital health initiatives to the solutions that were already available in their primary EHR platform. Not surprisingly, around a third of the initiatives were already available, and in many cases, they had been in deployment for a while. For health system CIOs, this is an ideal situation, considering that functionalities embedded in EHR systems often require minimal configuration to activate and no additional integration efforts, the latter being a significant selling point for going with the EHR platform for any new functionality. However, it is far from clear if existing solutions in an EHR system are the right choice for a given organization, despite the obvious advantages in speed of deployment and out-of-the-box integration. Daniel Barchi of New York–Presbyterian Hospital explains the typical trade-offs in such situations:

> There's probably a threshold for a tradeoff between something that is a 100-percent great stand-alone application versus something that is 70 percent as good using the

---

* Gawande, Atul. "Why Doctors Hate Their Computers." *The New Yorker.* November 12, 2018. Accessed December 13, 2019. www.newyorker.com/ma gazine/2018/11/12/why-doctors-hate-their-computers.

functionality of the EMR system. The 70-percent solutions embedded in the EMR system might beat the 100-percent stand-alone solution because of the ease of working and the idea that everything that is done in the core system interfaces with everything else. So not only does it benefit the clinician who is using that tool, but the EMR tool is also integrated in the seamless care of patients, end to end.

For the foreseeable future, EHR systems will continue to dominate the health system landscape. Healthcare CIOs must build robust capabilities to evaluate and compare EHR systems with emerging solutions from the rest of the technology vendor ecosystem. At a minimum, they must invest in internal capabilities to work with data from multiple systems and embrace an API-led approach to application development that delivers a fast time to market and improves developer satisfaction. They must embrace cloud-enabled models for scale and flexibility. They must recognize that digital health is about designing superior experiences and embrace best practices from technology firms as well as their peer organizations within and outside healthcare.

For their part, major EHR providers, notably Cerner and Allscripts, are embarking on aggressive acquisitions to bolster their product portfolios, expand their client footprint, and remain the dominant technology partners in the digital era, while partnering selectively with big tech firms for specific enhancements such as cloud enablement of the core transaction platforms. However, acquisitions can be tricky – consider Allscripts' acquisition of Practice Fusion, which ran into regulatory issues* – just as it can be risky for health systems to continue to rely on a single dominant vendor relationship.

---

* "Allscripts' Practice Fusion Subpoenaed over Alleged HIPAA, Kickback Issues." *Modern Healthcare*. May 7, 2019. Accessed December 13, 2019. www.modern healthcare.com/technology/allscripts-practice-fusion-subpoenaed-over-allege d-hipaa-kickback-issues.

As John Glaser, former CIO of Partners HealthCare who has also served as an Executive Vice President with Cerner, points out, "EHR companies have to be careful about assuming they can do it all by themselves." For EHR vendors, this presents a conundrum: In the absence of continued value creation and growth, Custodians can also lose relevance over the long term.

Enablers: Rent It, Build on It

Enablers are the most highly represented category of technology providers in the healthcare IT ecosystem today. This category includes big technology platform firms, such as Google, Microsoft, Apple, and Salesforce, that have built technology stacks that integrate multiple emerging and traditional data sources, including EHR systems. A large number of emerging digital health solutions are also essentially enabling platforms; they do not necessarily provide a point solution to a problem but provide a platform that enables health systems to build solutions for the problems. Enabler platforms want to be seen as extensible platforms that can be applied to a range of problems.

Major technology firms have also built a broad and deep range of products that have become standard enterprise software. Microsoft's Office 365 and Salesforce's customer relationship management (CRM) platform are examples. Google, Microsoft, and Amazon have become the de facto platforms of choice for cloud hosting services. Some firms have taken the concept of cloud-hosted software and built what are referred to as health clouds, which are purpose-built stacks for the healthcare industry. Health clouds include built-in integration features, security features that comply with the healthcare industry's requirements for patient medical information, and advanced analytics capabilities that can deliver insights through AI and machine-learning algorithms that run on the data hosted in their cloud environments. While the big technology firms may not be as deeply entrenched as Custodians within client environments, they have deep experience in building and deploying enterprise technology platforms at scale. What they may be lacking in depth of knowledge about clinical workflows, they more than make up for with advanced technology architectures, providing rich development environments for innovators to create last-mile solutions using open APIs.

Judging by the success of a handful of EHR firms in dominating the health system landscape over the past decade for transactional systems, is it possible that healthcare may be headed for an era of platform domination in digital health? In most other industries, notably consumer industries, a handful of platforms have emerged as winner-take-all models, notably social media (Facebook), search advertising (Google), and e-commerce (Amazon). Platform technologies have revolutionized industry after industry with one big exception: healthcare. We have outlined a few reasons why this may be.

Most platforms fail, regardless of the sector they operate in. A study of 250 platforms, published* in the *Harvard Business Review*, provides a sobering view of the prospects for platforms in general. For every Uber and Airbnb that goes for world domination through "blitzscaling" and first-mover advantage, there are several that do not make it past their fifth anniversary. The reasons range from late entry to mispricing, lack of trust, and underestimating competition. Healthcare has historically been a low-trust economy, with payers, providers, and pharmaceutical companies in largely adversarial relationships in a zero-sum game. For platforms to succeed, market participants must share data and invest in collaborative initiatives to improve healthcare outcomes and reduce costs for the sector. The closest we have come to this

---

* Yoffie, David B., Annabelle Gawer, and Michael A. Cusumano. "A Study of More Than 250 Platforms Reveals Why Most Fail." *Harvard Business Review.* May 29, 2019. Accessed December 13, 2019. https://hbr.org/2019/05/a-study-of-more-than-250-platforms-reveals-why-most-fail.

ideal of data sharing for the public good in healthcare has been in health information exchanges, and even those have failed to gain traction due to a variety of issues.

Ideally, the COVID-19 pandemic has demonstrated the importance of platforms, enabling future focus and success.

Users are slow to adopt digital health platforms. For a platform economy to succeed, consumers have to use the platforms. Prior to the pandemic, even telehealth platforms, seen as a transformative way to deliver healthcare, are seeing relatively low adoption rates among physicians. The American Hospital Association has documented* the key issues, notably coverage and reimbursement by Medicare for telehealth visits. Despite the proliferation of digital health solutions, healthcare consumers are using digital health tools primarily for basic activities such as online health information and scheduling appointments, a relatively low threshold for measuring progress.[†] This suggests a gap between the billions spent by big tech firms on building platforms and the market's readiness for those platforms. Again, we may be witnessing a seismic, permanent pandemic inspired shift.

It is all about how to unlock the data. Healthcare IT has been bedeviled by interoperability challenges, when two systems cannot talk to each other due to the absence of a widely accepted format for information exchange. For now, the custodianship of the data rests with health systems and their EHR vendors. There is a growing activism about handing over the ownership of the data to consumers (including a proposed CMS rule[‡] that will make it mandatory for consumers to be provided access to all their medical information), but we are

---

* "Fact Sheet: Telehealth." American Hospital Association. Accessed December 13, 2019. www.aha.org/system/files/2019-02/fact-sheet-telehealth-2-4-19.pdf.

† Molla, Rani. "Mary Meeker's Most Important Trends on the Internet." *Recode.* June 11, 2019. Accessed December 13, 2019. www.vox.com/recode/2019/6/11/1 8651010/mary-meeker-internet-trends-report-slides-2019.

‡ "CMS Interoperability and Patient Access Proposed Rule." CMS.gov. March 4, 2019. Accessed December 13, 2019. www.cms.gov/Center/Special-Topic/Interop erability/CMS-9115-P.pdf.

still in early stages. Even if we were to solve the problems of secure and seamless data exchange among participants in the health IT ecosystem, there is a growing realization that the fundamental building block for driving innovation, namely, a universal patient identifier, does not exist (proposed legislation* could change that).

Technology firms and digital health innovators tend to look at healthcare from the outside and do not have an adequate appreciation of its unique nature. It is important for digital health innovators to get deeply involved in healthcare, so that they understand the intricacies of care delivery and design products accordingly. Big tech firms, for their part, have to overcome a general lack of trust by consumers to share personal medical information on their platforms. Google's challenge with public trust around the use of personal data was a major factor in the company's troubles over its data-sharing partnership with Ascension Health.†

Somewhere along the spectrum from cloud-only to on-premises-only solutions, health systems need to find ways to move forward with a strategy that addresses all the needs of a digital transformation roadmap. Health systems are already on the path of digital transformation. However, any decision to go with a health cloud platform starts with having a cloud strategy in the first place. Health clouds are not an instant solution for developing and deploying digital health solutions at scale, and there are significant differences among various players that have implications for the effort, costs, and timelines of an enterprise-level digital transformation platform.

* Landi, Heather. "House Votes to Lift Ban on Federal Funding for Unique Patient Identifier." Fierce Healthcare. June 13, 2019. Accessed December 13, 2019. www.fiercehealthcare.com/tech/house-votes-to-lift-ban-federal-funding-for-unique-patient-identifier.
† Copeland, Rob and Sarah E. Needleman. "Google's 'Project Nightingale' Triggers Federal Inquiry." *The Wall Street Journal.* Updated November 12, 2019. Accessed December 13, 2019. www.wsj.com/articles/behind-googles-project-nightingale-a-health-data-gold-mine-of-50-million-patients-11573571867.

Dr. Toby Cosgrove, an advisor to Google, suggests* that firms like Google need to focus on how to add applications on top of EHR systems and avoid trying to sell large cloud contracts to health systems. His comments suggest that health systems are ready for digital transformation but not quite prepared for a large-scale shift to the cloud. The reality is that one may not be possible without the other.

Our research indicates that the major technology firms are taking distinctly different approaches to the healthcare markets. Apple has a unique combination of hardware (smart devices) and software design capabilities that drive its healthcare market strategy. Among all the big players, Apple, with a strong B2C heritage and a deeply ingrained DNA of experience design, has probably made the most progress in creating an integrated ecosystem for personal health management, including data-sharing partnerships with over 100 healthcare providers at the time of writing. By integrating data from multiple sources and allowing patients to track their health through intuitive iOS apps and devices, Apple has created a strong connection with healthcare consumers who use their iPhones to access all manner of services. Microsoft, on the other hand, is more known for its enterprise B2B relationships across all sectors, including healthcare. With its existing enterprise footprint, a focus on the Azure cloud platform with machine-learning capabilities, a slew of research partnerships, and high-profile leadership hires, Microsoft has strong mindshare with healthcare CIOs. Amazon and Apple are also getting directly into the business of healthcare services. In addition to its participation in Haven Healthcare (a joint venture with JP Morgan Chase and Berkshire Hathaway), Amazon is also setting up its own clinics as well as using its e-commerce platform to get into the sales and distribution of

* Ellison, Ayla. "Toby Cosgrove's Advice for Google's Cloud Team." *Becker's Hospital Review.* November 5, 2018. Accessed December 13, 2019. www.becker shospitalreview.com/healthcare-information-technology/toby-cosgrove-s-advic e-for-google-s-cloud-team.html.

pharmaceutical and medical products. Amazon's purchase of online pharmaceutical retailer PillPack for over $750 million in 2018* was notable because it put a major tech firm directly in the business of healthcare products and services.

Among other big tech firms, Salesforce leads with its CRM approach to enabling patient and caregiver experiences. Google, on the other hand, with its somewhat dispersed portfolio of healthcare initiatives across parent company Alphabet's portfolio – Verily, Calico, DeepMind, and Google Cloud – is taking a multipronged approach to achieve success at any cost in healthcare. Microsoft and Salesforce have also invested in building a partner ecosystem, which has produced many promising digital health start-ups that deliver innovative last-mile experiences. Salesforce's $6.5 billion acquisition of integration software provider MuleSoft† may turn out to be a key advantage as healthcare data gets unlocked through SMART on FHIR applications.‡

Several major technology firms have launched health clouds in an effort to build a comprehensive digital health platform for the future. In choosing to go with a health cloud platform, health system CIOs have to carefully evaluate the value proposition along a few important dimensions. Table 6.1 provides a high-level set of criteria for assessing health cloud providers.

Healthcare has a last-mile problem, which is a lack of adequately proven and tested point solutions that address specific patient or caregiver needs. EHR vendors have built several solutions (such as online scheduling and messaging)

---

* Farr, Christina. "The Inside Story of Why Amazon Bought PillPack in Its Effort to Crack the $500 Billion Prescription Market." CNBC.com. May 10, 2019. Accessed December 13, 2019. www.cnbc.com/2019/05/10/why-amazon-bought-pillpack-for-753-million-and-what-happens-next.html.

† Miller, Ron. "18 Months After Acquisition, MuleSoft Is Integrating More Deeply into Salesforce." TechCrunch. November 19, 2019. Accessed December 13, 2019. https://techcrunch.com/2019/11/18/18-months-after-acquisition-mulesoft-is-integrating-deeper-into-salesforce/.

‡ "SMART App Launch Framework." HL7.org. Accessed December 13, 2019. www.hl7.org/fhir/smart-app-launch/.

Table 6.1   Evaluation framework for health cloud solutions

Criteria	Considerations
Healthcare focus	Healthcare is seen as a huge opportunity, and almost every major tech firm has declared an interest in healthcare. However, many firms merely look at healthcare as another segment in which to sell their standard offerings. Even within the firms that understand healthcare, their focus and approach depend on their heritage. For example, Salesforce brings a CRM-oriented approach, while GE Healthcare brings its deep domain knowledge in medical images
Features	The features of cloud platforms reflect the firm's core capabilities and areas of focus. While core platform features such as data security standards, middleware, and integration are part of every platform, some features are unique to some firms. As an example, Microsoft and Google provide advanced analytics tools and machine-learning algorithms for which they are seen as best-in-class
Pricing models	No two firms are the same when it comes to pricing, and this is potentially one of the big challenges in evaluating health clouds. Pricing models vary widely not just among the health cloud providers, but also within an individual platform. A health cloud platform may comprise hundreds of individual tools, and features and metering may be per-second, per-minute, per-hour, per-device, per-seat, and more. Estimating usage levels can be a challenge, especially if it is not clear what tools will be required for a specific application
Customer base	While many of the big tech firms have a large customer base of healthcare enterprises, the number of health cloud clients may be small. Health systems must look for health cloud platform implementation reference points before considering a health cloud

(*Continued*)

Table 6.1 (Continued)   Evaluation framework for health cloud solutions

Criteria	Considerations
Partner network	Health cloud providers have to work closely with leading EHR vendors to be able to access patient data. At the same time, they also have to onboard digital health start-ups by encouraging and motivating them to build solutions on their platforms. System integrators may also be required to put the pieces together. In the absence of a robust partner network, health cloud providers may end up transferring many of these responsibilities to health systems that must bear the additional costs of integration, vendor management, and governance
Leadership	The healthcare practices of many technology firms are often in name only. The strong indicators of their commitment to healthcare are their organizational structure, dedicated team sizes, and whether healthcare is treated as a strategic, stand-alone business. The size and experience of the leadership matters as well, including whether the leadership includes senior executives with clinical backgrounds

Source: Damo Consulting Inc.

as part of their overall platform offering. Big tech firms, on the other hand, are relying largely on digital health start-ups and internal IT organizations within healthcare organizations to build the last-mile solutions by using a health cloud or another enterprise-class software platform. By exposing underlying data assets through APIs, health cloud platform providers are creating a framework for developers to take advantage of all the components of the health cloud stack to compose and deploy new applications quickly. Seizing the opportunity, an entire generation of cloud-only start-ups is leading the charge for innovation in healthcare, using human-centered design to build digital experiences from the ground up, fueled by billions in venture capital. This new generation of digital health innovators is the focus of the next section.

Arbitrageurs: We Can Do It Cheaper, Faster, and Better

Arbitrageurs are the final category of technology providers in our technology vendor assessment framework. Arbitrageurs are firms that rely on human expertise, scale, and locational advantages to deliver their services. Arbitrageurs include technology-agnostic consulting firms, such as Accenture and Deloitte as well as India-heritage firms such as Tech Mahindra, Wipro, and Infosys, that rely on highly skilled technology talent and leverage labor-arbitrage models with offshore teams. By virtue of their broad technology capabilities, Arbitrageurs can deliver on everything from building digital health applications to implementing and managing underlying technology infrastructure. While the firms mentioned above rely on labor cost arbitrage, there are other forms of arbitrage as well. The most important of these is scale, exemplified best by firms such as Amazon, Google, and Microsoft that can, due to the scale of their operations, offer managed hosting services at a much lower cost and much higher reliability than can any individual healthcare enterprise. A final class of Arbitrageurs comprises boutique consulting firms that excel in specific skills that health systems can draw on to assist them in their digital transformation efforts – call them the knowledge Arbitrageurs. One of us (Paddy) runs a firm that provides digital transformation advisory services and acts as a strategic partner to CIOs and CDOs to bring expert knowledge and best practices in developing digital roadmaps and navigating the technology landscape.

It is important to note that there are existing expert resources within healthcare organizations already. Internal development teams bring a level of appreciation and knowledge of the needs of end users that can never be matched by external organizations. However, most organizations have a limited pool of internal resources and have to make strategic choices and trade-offs around what capabilities are best developed in-house and which can be sourced from the outside. Internal resources are best deployed to gain a deep and ongoing understanding and prioritization of stakeholder needs. They are the most knowledgeable about data sources and their applications in improving healthcare outcomes. Healthcare organizations must also address career aspirations for internal resources while ensuring that they learn and benefit from the best practices of external consulting firms. They must also decide what areas they need to exit from; for example, a scarcity of talent for legacy on-premises technologies and data center management implies a significant risk in terms of vendor support, talent flight, and increased costs.

The global IT services vendor landscape has evolved dramatically in the past couple of decades. The most remarkable development in the service provider landscape has been the emergence of major multinational firms from India, many of which are multi-billion-dollar enterprises employing hundreds of thousands of associates and serving thousands of customers in western nations. Indian firms such as Tata Consultancy Services (TCS), Infosys, and Wipro have relied on labor-arbitrage models for their success over the past 25 years, starting by helping western companies address the Y2K problem in the 1990s. Over time, these firms have built long-term relationships with their clients, often signing long-term contracts to manage IT operations using low-cost resources and infrastructure in India. Many of these firms have evolved along with changing technology trends to develop strong capabilities in emerging tech areas such as cloud and AI, organically and through acquisitions. Global consulting firms based in the United States and Europe, for their part, have moved in the reverse direction, setting up large operations teams in India, the Philippines, and low-cost locations in Eastern Europe and South America to tap into talent pools and compete with Indian firms on price. More recently, some end customers, especially in banking and insurance, have decided to set up their own operations in India to take advantage of scale economies to reduce their costs even further and retain control over intellectual property.

In comparison to pharmaceutical companies or health plans, health systems have traditionally avoided entering into strategic partnerships with India-based firms. One of the major considerations has been concern around providing access to patient medical information to overseas firms with a perceived lack of governance around the handling of that information. In at least one high-profile incident, India-based TCS was sued by Epic for hundreds of millions of dollars* over the mishandling of intellectual property by a TCS employee. The case was winding its way through the courts at the time of writing.

Firms that rely on India-based resources often have to contend with restrictions on work visas for associates to be deployed on short-term projects in the United States. Tightening restrictions around the number of US work visas have upended the economic model for many firms. In response, many Indian IT services firms have started to invest heavily in setting up operations centers in the United States and hiring aggressively in the local markets to serve clients. Others such as Tech Mahindra, have acquired healthcare specific U.S. firms such as the HCI Group to overcome such challenges and gain immediate market presence and talent. Naturally, this shift has cost implications that impact the competitiveness of these firms. Global IT services firms have, for their part, recognized that years of growth have led to redundant layers of middle management in many of these service

---

* Mendonca, Jochelle. *Tata Consultancy Services' $420 Million Trade Secrets Case Moves to Higher Court.* March 25, 2019. Accessed January 29, 2020. https://ec onomictimes.indiatimes.com/tech/ites/tata-consultancy-services-420-million-trade-secrets-case-moves-to-higher-court/articleshow/68554532.cms.

provider firms, and the forces of automation have created pricing and margin pressures. One of the major firms, Cognizant, announced layoffs of over 7,000 employees in November 2019 as part of a "cost structure optimization"* that involved redirecting other roles into further opportunity areas such as data management and digital transformation. All in all, 2 percent of the workforce of nearly 300,000 was expected to be impacted by the exercise. Other firms are following suit.

IT services firms are also repositioning themselves in the emerging demand environment where skills related to digital technologies such as user experience design, cloud migration, artificial intelligence, and robotic process automation have risen significantly. Over the past few years, many of these firms have increased acquisitions to consolidate their presence in a particular segment (e.g., Cognizant's acquisition of Trizetto for the payer space) or to gain a foothold in a new market (e.g., Wipro's acquisition of HealthPlan Services). Consolidation within the IT service provider space is also picking up as firms try to bulk up in response to industry consolidation and pricing pressures on the client side. DXC's acquisition of Luxoft, NTT Data's acquisition of Dell Services, and Atos's acquisition of Syntel were all multi-billion-dollar transactions that have reshaped the companies significantly. Most global IT services firms also continue to invest in tuck-in acquisition to build specific competencies, especially in the digital space. Private equity firms have also swooped in to take majority stakes in mid-sized firms, looking presumably for a profitable exit after rationalizing costs and bulking up some more with the acquired firms.

Healthcare organizations must recognize the attributes and business models of global IT services in order to develop the appropriate types of partnerships. In general, the larger firms

---

* Panettieri, Joe. "Cognizant: Targeted Layoffs in 2019, Growth Acceleration in 2020?" ChannelE2E. November 1, 2019. Accessed December 13, 2019. www.channele2e.com/business/talent/cognizant-layoffs-2019-october/.

prefer to do larger deals that justify their overall cost structures and costs of new client acquisitions. Large global IT services firms, especially the ones with Indian heritage, also prefer multi-year deals, particularly if they leverage low-cost offshore resources to perform operational tasks such as IT infrastructure management, service desk management, and storage and network management. Legacy application support is another source of annuity revenue for many firms. A steady ongoing revenue stream from services delivered mostly by offshore resources that are significantly lower cost than US-based technical staff has allowed many firms to build large cash reserves (local tax incentives for foreign exchange earnings have helped as well). The flip side is that many of these firms are not well set up to do smaller transactions, which is often where digital transformation projects lie. A number of smaller and more specialized firms have emerged in recent years with capabilities in a specific functional or technical area that offer viable alternatives to the larger firms.

The emergence of new technologies has significant implications for Arbitrageur firms and the enterprises they serve. An example of this is the rapid growth of cloud computing. CIOs and technology providers alike have had to redefine their operating models with cloud enablement at the core rather than at the periphery, as more and more enterprises reduce their data center footprint and shift workloads to the cloud. Even established technology firms that have long held onto the on-premises model of software deployment and management have repositioned their offerings on cloud platforms as SaaS. The stunning success of cloud computing over the past decade may be repeated in the future with other emerging technologies as well.

For IT service providers, the implications go beyond simply reskilling for the emerging technology landscape. As healthcare enterprises embark on digital transformation, ownership of digital initiatives and the IT budgets that enable the transformation may shift toward other stakeholders, notably the chief digital officer. IT firms, long used to working mainly within CIO organizations, will have to learn the language of healthcare in addition to the language of technology. Many emerging firms, and quite a few incumbent firms, are not well positioned to make this transition, relying on technical prowess and cost advantages for continued growth, even as the demand for traditional IT services to develop applications is replaced by ready-to-deploy cloud-based SaaS solutions that require little or no support. Many IT departments are reinventing themselves as orchestrators of technology rather than builders of homegrown technology solutions. Healthcare CIOs must carefully assess their incumbent relationships and identify new service providers that demonstrate the strongest alignment with the emerging digital health technology landscape.

What Successful Technology Vendors Do Right

Despite their stated commitment to customer success, many vendors are inconsistent and ineffective in their approach to client relationships. In the current competitive landscape, most technology business leaders are driven by top-line considerations and often lose sight of the need to strike a balance between patience and the pursuit of growth. Many large technology firms also tend to have organizational structures in which sales teams are tasked with new revenue targets that discourage teams from looking beyond the current or the next quarter. In one case, despite the vendor's global leadership position and best-in-class technology, the account executive (AE) on the ground repeatedly disregarded the client's expectations on the norms of engagement with stakeholders across the enterprise and eventually had to be removed. However, we have found that successful vendors do certain things right most of the time and do them more consistently than their less successful competitors.

Account management: Strategic partnerships rely on strong account leadership from vendor organizations, specifically the account executive. In consulting firms, this role is typically played by a client partner who is responsible for overall revenues from the account, but is also empowered to make decisions to serve the client's needs. While all AEs have revenue responsibilities, clients would prefer the AE not to be a salesperson whose primary responsibility is to close the sale and move on to the next deal. They should be a relatively senior executive with whom the client can develop a long-term primary relationship. If the owner of a strategic partnership is the CIO, the vendor AE should be at a peer level within their own organization. There have been several deals where the assigned AE is a frontline salesperson who is little more than a messenger with limited or no decision-making authority. It almost never works well. For truly strategic partnerships, it is best to work with peer equivalents who wield significant influence within their respective organizations and can navigate the politics and dynamics of both organizations to make the relationship successful. The AE is someone who must be there long past the sales cycle and next year's bonus.

Executive sponsorship: It is highly desirable to have an executive sponsor who is a senior executive within the vendor organization and who has financial authority, access to resources, and is individually invested in the success of the relationship. As a general rule, we recommend having direct access to the highest levels of decision-making in the technology partner organization and agreeing on a communication process and frequency at the outset, especially when the stakes are high. We prefer CEO-to-CEO pairings when possible. The higher the stakes, the more important it is to have direct access to the CEO. For smaller healthcare organizations, this may be impractical, but the goal remains the same. Find a senior executive from the vendor who is willing to get on calls, help direct the partnership, and remove barriers. If a vendor is unwilling to assign a senior executive, it is a clear sign that they do not view the organization or partnership as valuable.

Solution mindset: The best partnerships we have seen are those where the AEs know the business so well that they proactively bring new ideas and solutions. Successful AEs recognize a client's business needs and have the ability to mobilize internal resources to solve a problem, sometimes even when their company may not benefit immediately by way of incremental revenues or profits. The best AEs and vendor organizations will also go beyond near-term considerations to help clients through challenging periods. In one case we are familiar with, the health system was struggling on the revenue side of the business. The CEO of one of their strategic vendors convened an all-hands meeting, flying in key leaders to the client's headquarters to spend an entire day focused on finding ways to overcome immediate challenges. The only caveat is to be cautious that these solutioning interactions are not set up as blatant sales pipeline development exercises for the AE.

Pricing and terms: The most successful vendors are flexible and creative with commercial aspects of the engagement and are very effective at advocating on behalf of clients within their organizations to help structure win-win deals. Inflexibility in pricing or terms often kills partnerships despite strong teams and product offerings. In one case, the technology vendor's unwillingness to accept the major terms of a business associate agreement led to a collapse of negotiations and wasted time and effort all around, despite the merits of the product and the company. Vendors who demonstrate a lack of flexibility with pricing at the outset can be counted on to be the same way during the course of the relationship, often nickel-and-diming clients for all manner of services. In another example, a global tech firm that had signed a multiyear contract for outsourcing IT operations worth hundreds of millions of dollars assigned aggressive revenue growth targets to the AE on the ground. The AE decided that achieving the growth targets would be challenging due to contractual commitments to reduce year-on-year billings through productivity gains on the base level of services. The AE felt compelled to make up for the revenue shortfalls by charging for every service that was not explicitly covered in the contract, often bending the interpretation of contract language and overcharging for relatively minor services. It is hard to partner with a vendor that seems to have a one-sided view of the financials and is clearly taking advantage of the organization because they can.

Responsiveness and follow-through: Vendors with a strong customer service mindset will be very attentive and responsive to questions, requirements, and concerns. They are also very good at managing expectations and following-through on commitments. At one health system that signed a multi-year outsourcing contract worth hundreds of millions of dollars, the senior-most leaders from the vendor organization were based in Bangalore, India. During contract negotiations, the vendor established that they would be available at all hours of the day as needed for the success of the partnership. When serious performance issues emerged in the first year of the contract, the CIO of the health system was unable to get the kind of responsiveness and attention required to fix the issues quickly and could not get any senior executive from the vendor organization to make a personal visit to address the CIO's concerns. Paddy was called in by the CIO to work with stakeholders on both sides to bring the service levels back on track and renegotiate contract terms on behalf of the health system. The contract was restructured after several months of adversarial discussions, but by then the vendor had lost the trust of the client. Not long after the renegotiations were completed, the CIO of the health system decided to terminate the contract and award it to another vendor. It is important to note that not all failures in vendor relationships can be attributed to the vendor. Vendor relationships often go wrong due to unrealistic expectations by clients. By setting expectations clearly, understanding the vendor's motivations, and setting up relationships for mutual benefit, healthcare leaders can significantly accelerate their transformation journeys.

Key Takeaways and Action Steps

1. Healthcare executives must recognize that successful technology partnerships are a critical component of digital transformation. We recommend using our ICEA™ framework to categorize the technology vendors and evaluate each vendor within the categories.
2. Vendors often sit in more than one category in the ICEA™ model, especially larger technology firms. Health systems must make their partnership selection based on the primary role the technology vendor should play in the digital future of the enterprise.
3. Develop a structured evaluation model for digital health start-ups. Recognize that start-ups lack the financial resources to sustain extended sales cycles. Start with the end in mind. Ensure there is a pathway for enterprise-level adoption for start-up solutions that meet predetermined performance thresholds. Carefully assess the product maturity and additional efforts involved in customization and integrations as part of the total cost of ownership.
4. Leverage Arbitrageur firms to outsource parts of IT operations to low-cost offshore locations. Outsourcing selectively can release valuable internal resources for future-state initiatives.
5. Retreat idea: Convene a discussion to answer the following questions: With the digital strategy becoming increasingly clear, what partnerships should your organization consider? What partners do you have today? Who might be on your short list of partner candidates?

THIRTY-SECOND AGILE CONSULT

Volunteer to serve as a judge at a pitch day hosted by an incubator.

Chapter 7

Getting Digital Transformation Right

In the previous chapters, we have covered the digital transformation opportunity before us. We reviewed the long-term implications of the COVID-19 pandemic on how healthcare will be accessed and delivered in future. We considered the gap between current capabilities and those that healthcare enterprises need to invest in. We reviewed strategies to ensure you are prepared to leverage digital transformation today and far into the future. We shared a blueprint for success that can be modified to fit your organization. Based on agile principles, the blueprint allows you to take immediate control of your organization's destiny in this ever-changing climate of technology, reimbursement, and consumerism. We explained key structures and platforms you must build to ensure long-term success. Reviewing strategic enablers, we showcased several that you need to master on your journey to include emerging technologies. We focused at length on technology partnerships to ensure strong foundations and maximization of opportunities. With these critical pieces in place, we will spend the final section on the softer side of the success equation. Getting digital transformation right is much more than ensuring all platforms are in place and all key components are set. Rather, it is about the practical steps needed to begin: a focus on culture, partnerships, business cases, and finally managing risks.

Setting the Stage for Success

Our research and work with healthcare enterprises have revealed several best practices by digital transformation leaders who succeeded in gaining early traction and progressively won over their peers. Here are five important and timeless attributes spanning the impacts of consumerism, technology advancement and pandemic.

They have an enterprise vision and roadmap: Most healthcare enterprises today are implementing digital as standalone, often departmental programs. While this approach allows organizations to move faster, enterprise adoption becomes a challenge in the absence of an organizational champion with an overarching vision and a clear roadmap for implementation. The departmental/functional approach can also often create redundancies such as duplicate purchases of software licenses and suboptimal technology architecture choices. An enterprise digital roadmap streamlines and prioritizes initiatives across the organization, often by folding in existing investments into the roadmap, and ensures all-round alignment.

They involve stakeholders early: The most advanced digital transformation programs have involved cross-functional stakeholders early and given them an opportunity to weigh in with their expectations from digital transformation. Stakeholders appreciate the opportunity to have a voice in shaping the digital transformation vision and roadmap, and moreover provide valuable inputs on best practices at other enterprises in their fields. Early involvement also ensures stakeholder buy-in, which is critical for the success of the program. Following a transparent process for determining digital transformation priorities and inviting feedback from stakeholders are crucial for winning support and ensuring the successful implementation of digital programs.

They take inputs from their health system peers: Digital transformation leaders do not have the luxury of unlimited budgets or extended time frames to demonstrate results. Hence, they reach out to their peers in the industry to understand what has been working well. Peer group CIOs in healthcare are often willing to share their experiences, including successes and failures, that can be valuable reference points, especially if they are further along in digital transformation. Key aspects include technology architecture and vendor choices, best practices in experience design, and innovation management, to name a few. These inputs provide independent validation for the enterprise digital roadmap and win the confidence of stakeholders.

They try to replicate the successes from other industries: Many digital health start-ups featured in this book have taken inspiration from best practices in other industries. We found several digital transformation leaders, especially those that made the most progress with digital health initiatives, embraced best practices from consumer-oriented industries such as banking and online retailing. Big tech firms that work across all sectors have accumulated a wealth of best practices that can be readily applied in the healthcare context. Many CIOs and CDOs have invested in highly collaborative relationships with leading technology firms to benefit from their vast experience across other industries. Many health systems have gone one step further and hired senior executives with digital transformation experience from other sectors to infuse these best practices directly into the digital transformation roadmaps.

Selecting and Managing Your Technology Partners

Most organizations choose vendor relationships to advance their IT and digital health agendas. Some refer to vendors as partners, yet the relationship remains transactional. In unique circumstances, a win-win relationship is developed between supplier and customer. This is how we define partnership. We believe such a true partnership can help you accelerate digital transformation and at a better price point.

We first experienced the power of such a partnership several years ago. As a newly minted CIO for a prestigious academic health system, Ed inherited a telephone system that was fragmented and aged. This created an opportunity for digital transformation by leapfrogging traditional telephony models and building a first of its kind Voice over Internet Protocol (VoIP) phone system. This is mainstream today, but 15 years ago we were perhaps the first healthcare system in the world to deploy this. We could not afford to modernize our aging systems given the broken foundations of our network infrastructure. To build a converged network where voice, data, and video would become one required 100 M. We reached out to Cisco and caught the ear of their now Emeritus CEO John Chambers. In a meeting in his office, Ed complimented him for transforming the user experience of tens of thousands of concert-goers and sports fans, and pointed out that he now has the opportunity to make a real difference by applying Cisco's technology and know-how in healthcare to transform patient experiences. The message resonated. Cisco became a real partner and upgraded the health system's entire infrastructure at cost. In the process, Cisco gained its first healthcare customer to use their emerging tools. We have seen this approach replicated at several organizations with success. What we have described is one method to achieve the desired outcomes. You can leverage and adjust as it best fits your organization.

Partnerships do not always have to be about implementing new technologies. Often, large organizations benefit from outsourcing operational aspects to specialist global firms that can deliver the services better, faster, and cheaper, allowing CIOs to focus their energies and their most valued internal resources on future-state initiatives. Both of us have been intimately involved in large IT outsourcing transactions for the past two decades. Paddy has led global operations teams that have served as extended organizations for healthcare CIOs in strategic multi-year partnerships. Over time, these global operations teams have become strategic partners for the client's future-state initiatives by virtue of the deep knowledge and understanding they gain about the client's culture, processes, technologies, and business needs.

Building on the ICEA™ framework described in Chapter 6, we recommend you stratify all your vendors into one of four buckets: strategic, important, tactical, and emerging.

Strategic: We would limit this to three or four of your key vendors. These vendors are those whom you typically have a significant investment with and are key to running your organization. Your EHR vendor, for instance, might be one of your strategic partners. The CIO should own these relationships. Formal meetings are held quarterly with an annual review of the shared objectives and key results. Annual reviews should include the CEOs of both organizations. Convene a once a year day-long meeting with all the strategic partners. The forum allows the mutual exchange of information and future directions among the organizations. Half the day could be spent sharing your strategy for the forthcoming year and brainstorming among the partners on how they might work together to enable your organization's success.

Important: We would limit this next level of partnership to eight to ten vendors. These vendors also typically represent an area of heavy investment, but perhaps in a niche role. A cybersecurity tool vendor, for instance, might be an important partner. These relationships should be managed by your direct reports. As with strategic partners, there should be quarterly reviews of objectives and key results as well as an annual report card.

Tactical: This is where the largest number of your vendors will be categorized and managed. There should be an organizational owner for every vendor with at least an annual touchpoint. If there are unmanaged vendors, you likely are spending too much on their product or service. In fact, undertaking this process will expose significant waste and thus savings opportunities.

Emerging: Emerging vendors might be smaller but promising vendors such as start-ups. You will want to take a programmatic approach to these as well and keep an eye for how they might become tactical or strategic in the future. We have found that five to seven seems to be a manageable number. Again, you must use a disciplined approach to ensure value is attained: quarterly meetings with shared objectives and key results. Work closely with your innovation groups to gain early visibility to emerging solutions or platforms that could one day become an important partner to your organization.

As you look at your enterprise strategy and your current state, the opportunities for digital transformation will be self-evident. Once you have gone through the agile digital transformation blueprint described in Chapter 3, the gaps in your capabilities will show you what you need from your partners. In the ideal case, your strategic partners can work together to enable your digital transformation. If this is not the case or if you have not formalized such partnerships, you can follow the process we have described below to help you accomplish your goals:

■ **Assess what your current vendors can implement in your digital roadmap:** We believe in simplicity and have found that most organizations can create a single-slide artifact that can show the digital transformation roadmap highlighting the gaps to be filled. With the gaps identified, work with your strategic partners (if you have identified them) and key vendors to learn how they might help address the gaps. Take care to avoid introducing new vendors in an area where a current partner is already in the process of developing a product or service that will fill your gap. Conduct a couple of visioning sessions with the existing partners and share your digital roadmaps indicating the gaps to be filled. If the partner can address the majority of the gaps, build the partner into your digital transformation roadmap. If the existing partners are unable to fill the needs, initiate a market search for a digital transformation partner.

■ **Identify a strategic partner to implement the gaps in the roadmap:** With the roadmap in hand, and a clear understanding of what your current vendors can deliver, you can go to the marketplace and look for a vendor that might meet the majority of your gaps and be interested in a true strategic relationship. Ideally, this would be a transformative partnership where both parties can achieve success through a significant investment of time, leadership attention, and resources. Some argue that you should have multiple partners no matter what. We have found that having multiple strategic partners for a given area of work dilutes the potential for a special and differentiated relationship that can accelerate the transformation. One case where we initiated the search, we found three vendors who could each fill the majority of the gaps in the digital roadmap.

■ **Launch a formal selection process; look beyond product features and pricing:** In the example that we mentioned above, we considered multiple criteria in our evaluation. While we compared and contrasted products and services, these were largely even. Our primary focus was therefore on strategic alignment and cultural fit. Which company was headed in the same direction as us? Who had a similar vision? What were the core values? Which company was willing to take the highest risk toward an exclusive and truly transformative partnership? We also did not want this to be a trade of an exclusive vendor relationship for a deep discount on the price. In evaluating a partnership for the digital transformation of the enterprise, we looked for a partner whose CEO was willing to take the risk, co-invest, co-create, and be personally engaged in the success of the partnership. While teams did the side-by-side comparisons of financials and products and legal reviews were undertaken, our C-suites made trips to each other's organizations. We wanted to know each other as well as possible considering the gravity of the decision ahead of us. The visits also gave the potential partners an opportunity to learn more deeply about us. Everyone needs to go into such a relationship with eyes wide open. As with the vendor management framework, the success of such a partnership requires significant upfront and ongoing attention. Both sides agree to objectives and key results, and annual meetings rotate between headquarters. CEOs are engaged and kept informed of performance. With a rigorous selection process in place, the odds of success increase exponentially. There will always be unforeseen and unanticipated challenges that arise. You never want to use the contract to arbitrate a conflict. That is why the selection emphasis is largely on culture and fit. It will be these key relationships that help smooth out the rough waters when they occur. Do not select a company as a digital transformation partner because of a comparative product analysis or cost. Yes, they should inform the decision, but not make it.

■ **Manage your partnerships right:** Vendor relationships and vendor management are topics that merit their own book. Understand the business models and aspirations of the vendors who you choose to bring along on your digital transformation journey. Recognize that there are myriad factors that impact the success of a partnership. The nature of the product or solution and the financial stakes play a significant role in determining appropriate governance structures for different types of vendors. Successful partnerships require the parties to treat each other as in any serious relationship. There must be freedom of expression and freedom to speak truth; freedom to make mistakes and freedom to bring bold new ideas. Honesty and commitment are key components and hallmarks of successful partnerships.

Harnessing Innovation: Straddling Two Canoes

"Digital innovation is about finding new ways to solve existing problems," says Manu Tandon, CIO of Boston-based Beth Israel Deaconess Medical Center.

> To me digital innovation is an applied science. It is about making connections. It is about finding new ways to perform existing functions. It is about seeing a business problem from a 360-degree view, understanding the people, process and technology components that are playing into it and then creating a solution that leverages either new or sometimes traditional technologies in a new connected way.

While every health system is looking continually for innovation to improve care delivery and outcomes, for innovations to become part of the standard of care can be a long wait. Healthcare moves very slowly, and it does so for a number of reasons. It is challenging to introduce innovations and institute a new way of providing care when caregivers are already overwhelmed by the amount of time that they have to spend today on patient care and documenting the patient care in the EMR. In addition, when patient lives are involved, it tends to make healthcare providers cautious about how they adopt new technologies or approaches.

There is an unprecedented innovation opportunity in the digital transformation of healthcare and there is also a sense of urgency in moving toward a digital future, given the competitive environment, regulatory pressures, and the changing reimbursement models. In addition to traditional venture capitalists, we are seeing health systems getting into the innovation game themselves by setting up venture funds. Examples include Providence Health, Kaiser Permanente, Partners Healthcare, UPMC, Intermountain, and Mayo Clinic, to name but a few. Corporate venture capital (CVC) funds from several large health systems have been active in digital health, investing in promising start-ups, often through innovation funds and innovation centers that act as conduits for start-ups to gain access to clinical environments to build out products and platforms with active guidance and participation from clinicians. While these corporate venture funds are relatively small, the likelihood for promising start-ups with innovative solutions to accelerate the path to product validation and market acceptance improves with the support of a sponsoring health system.

At the heart of the innovation ecosystem are the healthcare enterprises. Leading health systems are innovating with health care delivery models and pricing/contracting models and are using technology to enable their digital transformation (Ed's book, *Voices of Innovation*, features several examples of how health systems are driving innovation). The accelerating pace of digital transformation and the disruptive potential of well-funded, large, non-traditional players from the tech and non-tech worlds entering healthcare has created a sense of urgency in health systems to accelerate innovation. The entry of technology giants such as Amazon with vast resources at their disposal has raised the stakes in the battle for the healthcare consumer. Health systems are increasingly compelled to adopt "no-regrets" strategies, making strategic bets on innovation and following-through to ensure joint success. However, health systems are caught between a rock and a hard place – the need to invest in innovation, but the lack of appetite for the risks and costs that come with it.

Karen Murphy of Geisinger Health System defines innovation as a fundamentally different approach to solving a problem that has *quantifiable outcomes*. Geisinger's Fresh

Food Farmacy* initiative uses population health analytics to identify type 2 diabetics with multiple chronic conditions and food insecurity for targeted interventions that deliver positive outcomes beyond what can be achieved through medication alone.

The use of patient data in the emerging models of commercializing innovation raises specific questions: Who owns the data? Who gets access to it? Who gets to share the benefits when the data gets monetized?

Healthcare enterprises, looking to augment revenue streams, evidently benefit from offering their data sets for hire. Creating a framework to allow digital innovation to be tested and piloted within their environments using their data also potentially provides early visibility to new ideas that can be deployed enterprise-wide. A few of these ideas may even be worthy of strategic investments with potentially big payoffs down the road. These alternative revenue streams are increasingly becoming part of the core business model for traditional healthcare enterprises. Many health systems have clear commercialization goals in mind for their innovation programs. Some are looking at innovation programs as incubators for commercially viable products, whereas others are looking to co-develop solutions for benefiting their patient populations in the short term. In all cases, their patient data and medical histories – in some cases, going back decades – are essential to the success of their innovation programs.

Digital health innovators and start-ups that come up with new ways to solve existing problems or find solutions to new problems face a big challenge: access to real-world data and an opportunity to validate the solution in a real-life clinical environment. Having the option to partner with a health plan or health system for access to data and a real-world environment accelerates the product development life cycle

---

* "Fresh Food Farmacy." Geisinger. Accessed December 13, 2019. www.geisinger.org/freshfoodfarmacy.

for start-ups. It also increases the chances of attracting venture capital investment, including from their sponsor enterprises. It does not hurt if the innovation partnership turns into a commercial relationship for the product or solution.

Healthcare consumers, whose data is powering these new business models, may well be asking themselves how any of these models benefits them directly. Notwithstanding the clarification that healthcare data belongs to the consumers by the Center for Medicare and Medicaid Service (CMS), the federal agency that oversees much of healthcare policy, there is no indication that the entities controlling and monetizing the data have an explicit compensation model in place to share the benefits accruing from these programs. The assumption is that the innovations emerging from these programs will indirectly benefit consumers through better quality and lower costs of care.

Due to restrictions on the use of HIPAA-protected patient data, providing access to the data for commercial ventures comes with several regulatory challenges and disclosure requirements. Consumers and regulators are increasingly raising questions about adequate disclosures on data sharing by health systems that may indicate rising advocacy for patients to have a bigger say in the sharing of their personal medical data as well as the monetization of their data. We are in the early days of data aggregation and monetization in healthcare. The public outrage over a partnership between Google and Ascension Health – which triggered a federal inquiry* – providing Google with access to millions of patient records without explicit permission from patients or their caregivers is an indication of how sensitive the sharing of personal medical information can be. Those who have the data are often loath to share it for a variety

---

* "Google's 'Project Nightingale' Triggers Federal Inquiry." WSJ. Accessed December 13, 2019. www.wsj.com/articles/behind-googles-project-nightingale-a-health-data-gold-mine-of-50-million-patients-11573571867.

of reasons. Alternative models are emerging. An initiative* at Stanford University directly offers consumers the opportunity to sell their healthcare data and has even come up with a differential pricing model based on the value of the data for research and innovation. However, "trading" healthcare data can also lead to unintended consequences, if secondary uses of the data lead to discriminatory practices if it falls into the wrong hands, for which there is limited or no legal and federal protection for consumers.†

Health systems across the nation are competing today on quality and price. The quality of the care and the price at which it is delivered are under scrutiny. Health systems have, by and large, exhausted the toolbox of traditional methods of lowering cost and improving quality. The patient experience of care and the patient's ability to access care at a time and modality of their choosing, not to mention transparency in the costs of care, are driving competition and a transformation of the healthcare business. Technology-led innovation is no longer an option, but a necessity for health systems trying to break out of the downward spiral. However, the continuing hold of fee-for-service in payment models has implications for the adoption of technology-led innovation in health systems. In the inevitable shift toward value-based care, health systems relying on fee-for-service face shrinking operating margins that impose severe limits on the enterprise's ability to fund innovation programs. Many health systems are therefore stuck in a "two-canoe" syndrome – clinging to the safety of assured revenue streams through fee-for-service while trying to transition to value-based care without putting the business at risk.

Regardless of how the organizational and innovation models play out, health systems have to eventually step off one of

---

* "AI Needs Your Data – And You Should Get Paid for It." WIRED. Accessed December 13, 2019. www.wired.com/story/ai-needs-data-you-should-get-paid/.
† Klosowski, Thorin. "What to Consider Before Trading Your Health Data for Cash." November 20, 2019. Accessed December 13, 2019. https://thewirecutter.com/blog/what-to-consider-before-trading-your-health-data-for-cash/.

the canoes and commit to a single way forward. Clearly, that path points in the direction of value-based care as the payment model of the future. Health systems that are already in fully capitated environments have to find ways to innovate while "keeping the lights on." At Johns Hopkins Medicine, which is essentially in a capitated model of payment due to the tight controls on reimbursements by the state of Maryland, CTO Dwight Raum leverages innovation opportunities to drive operating efficiencies and uses the incremental savings to fund further innovation. It's a model that might well serve health systems which still have a runway left with fee-for-service models today.

Funding Your Digital Transformation Journey

The price tag attached to digital transformation can run into hundreds of millions of dollars for a large health system. Based on our discussions with healthcare leaders as well as on publicly available information, we estimate that a budget allocation of a quarter to one half of a percentage of enterprise revenues is a benchmark number for digital transformation programs. For an enterprise with $10 billion in revenues, that translates to somewhere between $25 million and $50 million, spread over a three to five-year time frame depending on strategic priorities. With a net profit margin in the region of 2 percent of revenues, there is little margin for error with investments in the equation. Healthcare enterprises must therefore follow a structured approach to investment decisions based on a clear understanding of enterprise needs, a thorough understanding of the technology architecture choices, and deep insights on the technology solution provider landscape. With the recent pandemic, many organizations invested significantly more to immediately upgrade their infrastructure and enable virtual care. We expect to see this level of investment sustained for the next couple years in order to fill the gaps that were demonstratively exposed.

Most digital leaders secure funding commitment from an annual budget that can be deployed in implementing the roadmap in a carefully planned and phased manner. As part of the plan, digital transformation leaders also need to address technical debt as well as "game-changing" investments that would lay the foundation for the digital future of the enterprise.

While health systems are no strangers to substantial IT investments (considering the tens and hundreds of millions spent over the past decade on just implementing EMR systems), the crucial difference is that EHR systems were paid for through federally funded Meaningful Use incentives. There is no such incentive for digital health innovation. For us, this means that digital health innovation programs have to meet stringent financial criteria to obtain funding approvals, and also compete with other IT and non-IT enterprise priorities for a slice of the funding pie. Many digital innovation programs thus end up starting with a very focused set of initiatives and demonstrate tangible returns before qualifying for additional investments.

While this incremental approach is not our recommended approach for enterprises looking to transform their enterprises, we recognize organizational reality. We recommend enterprises make the investment in developing a multi-year roadmap against which individual initiatives can be implemented and monitored and will eventually lead to the implementation of the overall strategy and roadmap. Developing a digital roadmap also enabled leaders and stakeholders at large to get a good handle on the moving parts: the digital innovation priorities, the technology solutions landscape, internal capabilities, and funding considerations. We realize that digital transformation is in early stages and there is no template out there for a robust and proven digital transformation roadmap, especially for something as comprehensive in scope and scale as what we are outlining in this book. Each health system has to develop its roadmap based on its own unique set of priorities and challenges.

Allocating limited resources is a key role of leaders. Regardless of organizational reporting hierarchies and target operating models, investments should be carefully weighed and considered. Alignment with the entire organizational strategy is paramount. There must be a single governing body for clear decision-making that includes funding. We recommend the C-suite act as the IT steering committee (ITSC) (or digital steering committee) that is responsible for governance including demand management. When the IT steering committee reports elsewhere, its power and influence is diminished, and digital transformation will be at greater risk. Again, if your model has governance decisions flowing via the CDO, the same principles and structure apply.

When it comes to digital transformation, understanding total investments is critical. A commonly used approach that analyst firm Gartner recommends is simple to create and monitor: Divide IT spend into three buckets – Run, Transform, and Grow. You can create your own as long as they are well defined. Most organizations average 90/5/5. Progressive organizations continually push down Run while increasing Transform and Grow. One organization we served started at 90/5/5 and over the course of several years settled at 70/12/8. Our objective was to push to 50 percent Run. Only then does IT become truly strategic.

It is critical to take the time and create buckets of spend important to your organization. Using your IT steering committee, determine what targets you should have over the next several years. As you approach demand management, make sure all requests are tagged using your specific spend categories. This will simplify processes and make saying no to ideas easier. The relationship between governance and strong financial management through technology business management (TBM) will become abundantly clear and reinforce data-based decisions. The more business logic you can use, the less reliance your organization will have on emotional decisions that may be strategically misaligned.

Many IT and digital leaders we talked to, especially among the regional and mid-sized healthcare enterprises, expressed concern about the magnitude of the task at hand and the lack of adequate financial support for funding large-scale digital transformation initiatives. We acknowledge that healthcare is somewhat more resource-constrained than other sectors. However, digital leaders have no choice but to become creative and operate in a "two-speed" model, which requires them to do more every passing year while ensuring that they are "keeping the lights on." In addition to formal budget allocations, there are several ways to fund digital initiatives. Ed's example above is one where a major technology vendor (Cisco) agrees to underwrite some of the costs of a transformation program in a mutually beneficial relationship. Many start-ups in early stages are willing to deploy their solutions at cost, in return for an opportunity to validate their solutions in a real-life environment. At one health system, the innovation group constantly made carefully selected bets on technology solutions where the savings and benefits from the early stages of adoption would be reinvested back into an enterprise-wide rollout, with no additional funding requirements. Finally, we have discussed in length alternative revenue sources that can accrue from licensing access to data, offering consulting services, or selling internally developed solutions to other health systems.

Here is a major challenge that is one part financial and one part cultural. This challenge alone accounts for a primary reason healthcare remains behind peer industries related to digital transformation: our legacy financial thinking that is risk averse, capital based, long-term depreciation versus fail fast operational expense. In the digital age, we cannot rely on proformas where we try to maximize asset value over long periods of time. This encourages months-long, if not years-long building of business cases. It requires three- to five-year technology plans when we need to be agile and nimble and respond to market opportunities in weeks if not days. We must become comfortable with trusting instincts and gut feelings. We must become comfortable with trying new things that might fail and be okay with that. We must stop being punitive when models do not perform as expected. Our financial thinking must change to enable digital transformation.

The COVID-19 pandemic has made many hospitals financially vulnerable. The pressure to eliminate costs while enabling digital transparency will remain acute. On one hand IT will be challenged to significantly reduce costs while on the other hand, manage increased investment in digital capabilities. This balancing act will determine success or failure.

Managing Governance, Culture, and Change

Healthcare CIOs across the board are deeply involved in enterprise digital transformation today, with many either carrying the additional responsibility of chief digital officer or transitioning into the role full-time. However, digital transformation is more about culture change than about technology. While digital transformation is primarily IT-enabled, it is not the same as IT-led.

The target operating model of a digital transformation program is an essential determinant of success. There are three basic governance models that enterprises can choose from, as discussed here.

Centralized: In the centralized model, the digital function and resources are organizationally structured as an operating unit such as a Digital Center of Excellence (COE). The COE drives the execution roadmap, controls funding, and drives policy. This is the dominant model in healthcare organizations today. This approach can deliver the most optimal use of resources and drive rapid enterprise-wide adoption; however, decision-making can be slow and departmental priorities may be neglected.

Decentralized: In the decentralized model, individual departments or functions autonomously drive digital transformation. This approach delivers near-term results; however, it can result in operational inefficiencies and higher overall costs through duplicate spending and the absence of scale economies.

Hybrid: As the name suggests, a hybrid model combines elements of centralized and decentralized approaches. With a strong digital leadership at the corporate level, a hybrid approach can deliver the benefits of centralized policy, technology selection, and architectural standards while maintaining the autonomy and agility of individual groups. We see health systems where multiple digital initiatives may already be underway at departmental and functional levels; however, it is also the case that in these enterprises, there is no centralized digital function.

One of the fundamental challenges for a digital transformation leader is to recognize that ownership for success with digital programs lies with key stakeholder groups in the organization. Clinical and nursing operations, revenue cycle management, and patient experience are some of the prominent stakeholder groups who have a stake in the digital transformation of their functional areas. CIOs who lead digital transformation must take pains to ensure that enterprise digital transformation is not seen as an "IT" initiative – or at least, not just an IT initiative. Digital transformation depends on a range of interconnected programs within an enterprise. These include enterprise data management, enterprise analytics, patient experience, population health management, and innovation, to name but a few. Rarely do all these programs lie within one function such as IT.

Given that digital transformation is in early stages in healthcare, the organization models for assigning ownership for implementing digital roadmap also vary widely across

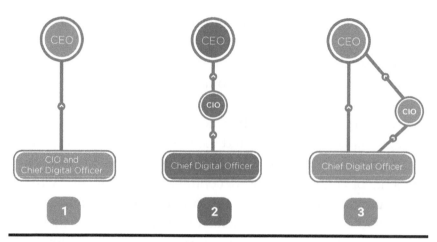

Figure 7.1   The role of the chief digital officer in healthcare organizations

enterprises. Figure 7.1 indicates where the role of the chief digital officer sits in different health systems today. However, healthcare is in the early stages of maturity when it comes to defining the chief digital officer role and function.

Aaron Martin, Chief Digital Officer of Providence Health, says:

> In healthcare, you see much more that the CDO and CIO roles are kind of combined. But I think as health systems and insurers start to understand that these are very different problems to solve, you will start to see the Chief Digital Officer get separated from the CIO role. CIOs require a very different set of skills around how to deliver technology at a massive scale, deal with serving employees, dealing with massive amounts of enterprise data and then managing very complex relationships with technology partners who are helping with these issues. So that's kind of how it nets out outside of health care and we will see what healthcare does with it.

Regardless of reporting relationships, chief digital officers are required to gain cross-functional alignment for success with implementing digital roadmaps and demonstrating sustained value with digital programs. The digital function also often intersects with other emerging functions within the healthcare enterprise today. Here are some examples.

Enterprise analytics: While analytics often sits in the IT function, it is just as often a stand-alone enterprise function or an enterprise function that sits inside another, such as the CFO organization. Even within the definition of enterprise analytics, routine reporting for quality metrics may sit in one function, while advanced analytics that focuses on building artificial intelligence (AI) and machine-learning tools may be led by a chief analytics officer (CAO). The CAO works independently with stakeholder groups to identify use cases and integrate them into clinical or operational workflows.

Enterprise data management: Ownership of enterprise data and the management of the data could sit in different parts of the enterprise. CIOs usually have the ownership of core data sets such as EHR data but may not have ownership or control of other data sets. An example would be third-party consumer data, which is licensed and used primarily for marketing. Further, the ownership of the data may lie within a function, while the responsibility for the infrastructure to host and manage the data may be part of the CIO organization. The advanced analytics function responsible for developing predictive models on patient health outcomes may sit in yet another part of the enterprise.

Patient experience: Many health systems have appointed chief patient experience officers, and the role often reports directly to the CEO. The patient experience officer's role involves creating alignment across the various functions that touch the patient during various stages of their journey – such as marketing, patient visits, payment, and collections – and requires IT-enablement to streamline the workflows and create superior experiences for the patient.

Innovation: Many healthcare enterprises have set up innovation groups that are typically stand-alone organizations tasked with a range of objectives such as fostering and com-mercializing innovations, creating and promoting innovation ecosystems, and, increasingly, generating new revenue streams through equity participation and royalty agreements. Given these objectives, the chief innovation officer often has a set of goals that do not directly align with enterprise digital transformation. However, innovation groups can be great sources of new ideas and solutions for reimagining patient and caregiver experiences and therefore a critical enabler for digital transformation.

Other aspects that impact enterprise digital transformation include departmental purchase of IT solutions (shadow IT as it is often referred to) and lack of standardization of technology platforms (often exacerbated by M&A activity), to name just a couple. Notwithstanding the variations in organizational models, several technology components required for enterprise digital transformation sit in the CIO organization today. These include enterprise IT infrastructure, core applications, information security, and systems integration. While CIOs have taken on the mantle of chief digital officers in many healthcare enterprises, the role of chief digital officer is emerging as one that requires cross-functional expertise – innovation management and experience design – that is characteristic of systems of engagement that directly impact revenues and customer satisfaction.

The healthcare sector is in the early stages for a digital transformation process and strategy. As pointed out in an earlier chapter, there are very few dedicated chief digital officer roles today, and in most cases, the role is assumed to be part of the CIO. In some cases, the CIO is transitioning to a chief digital officer role. What is really important is that there is awareness that the changing needs of the customer must be met and healthcare as an industry has to make it as easy, smooth, and frictionless as possible for customers to be able to access healthcare services. If traditional health systems fail to deliver improved service, a new set of competitors will certainly step in to fill the gap and take the market. Health systems have to be cognizant of the changing marketplace dynamics, and at the same time have a methodical approach to digital strategy where the business is very much involved in the entire evaluation and prioritization of projects in an enterprise digital roadmap.

Regardless of who leads, there must be alignment with IT. In one health system we are familiar with, the CDO function was mandated to develop innovative digital experiences for patients. The group had built a stand-alone organization and invested in a separate set of technology platforms to serve its needs. Many of these platforms were enterprise-class back-end platforms that had little to do with developing innovative experiences and more to do with enabling productivity or managing IT environments. Consequently, there was a significant amount of overlap and friction with the CIO organization resulting in a lack of alignment with organizational priorities, suboptimal use of technology resources, mistrust, and unhealthy internal competition for business. We have seen organizations where there is complete alignment between CDO and CIO, despite independent lines of reporting relationships to enterprise leadership. Based on our observations and experience, we recommend that the CIO must be central in digital transformation, either as the leader or reporting to the leader of the enterprise digital transformation effort. No one can serve two masters. Creating a two-headed monster, no matter the resolve, will lead to fragmentation and silos. Digital transformation will be slowed by competing agendas and duplication of scarce resources.

Addressing Cultural Aspects of Transformational Programs

Every organization has its own culture, so even the most well-crafted strategy and the corresponding platform are at risk of failure if not accounted for. The best antidote to having a transformation of any kind derailed is to listen to dissenting voices. One of the Epic healthcare technology failures happened at Cedars-Sinai in Los Angeles in 2002. Despite solid technology and all the requisite planning for success, two physicians led a revolt that would force administration to abandon the project. It would be a couple more years before Cedars would try again, this time with success. One of Ed's formal mentors at University Hospitals Health System (UHHS) in Cleveland has retold the story several times. Tom Zenty had just left Cedars as their COO to become CEO of UHHS. Leading the selection of an EHR vendor and designing the implementation, Tom implored Ed to listen to every dissenting voice until all questions had been answered. The team did and UHHS had great success with their EHR.*

When we listen to the voice of the customer, we can make the mistake of only interviewing those in leadership. This is another trap. While it is critical to listen to formal leaders, it is equally important to listen to the "influentials": individuals who do not have a formal leadership title, but everyone follows their lead. You must open as many listening posts as possible and go out of your way to ensure everyone has a chance to share concerns or ideas. Some unique methods we have used include evening meet-ups at a local wine bar, early morning walks around campus, and collaborative rounding. We created ad hoc, short-term advisory teams to encourage even more voices. Before the digital strategy went to governance, over 500 clinicians and administrators had the opportunity to engage. We addressed every dissenting voice. When the strategy was presented, it was unanimously approved.

Now there is much more to culture than just listening. However, this is one aspect you cannot afford to ignore.

Managing change successfully: Most organizations have become adept with change management. Many employ

---

* Patient Safety Monitor. *Hospital's Failure with Electronic Medical Records a Caution for Others*. March 24, 2005. Accessed January 27, 2020. http://patients afetymonitor.com/Hospitals-failure-with-electronic-medical-records-a-caution-for-others/873-46239.

Kotter's "8-Step Process for Leading Change" and for good reason. People are familiar with the model and it works. You can choose any process or methodology your organization is most comfortable with but choose one and stick with it. Culture eats strategy for lunch. Let us dive into an example of how to leverage this framework.

Create a sense of urgency: Chapter 1 is replete with reasons why we need to digitally transform our enterprises. It is survival of the digital fittest: changes to reimbursement, a focus on wellness, and consumerism jump out. Throw in the need to address clinician burnout and improve the overall patient experience, and you have all the urgency required. Personalize this to your organization specifically and the competitive forces at play in your market.

Build a guiding coalition: With your IT steering committee granting you the authority, build out a structure that ensures all voices are heard and all ideas recorded. If the ITSC is not chaired by the CEO (as recommended), be sure there is an enterprise announcement and physical kick-off where the CEO publicly recognizes your digital leadership. You need this mantle of authority for success. Beneath the ITSC we created a digital steering committee that focused exclusively on digital transformation. Everything in this process is temporary to guard against bureaucracy. For each specific strategy, a subcommittee was created focusing specifically on that journey. For instance, we identified caregivers as a separate and distinct journey. The subcommittee was populated based on specialization. With this structure, we were able to build a coalition of 500 formal and informal leaders of our organization. As inclusivity increases, risk decreases.

Form a strategic vision: For visions to be effective and inspiring, they must be bold. At the Cleveland Clinic, the pre-pandemic vision became "50% of OP visits are virtually 25% IP days at home." With the vision tested and approved, we developed corresponding initiatives. Everyone was on notice that the way we practiced medicine would forever be changed.

Enlist a volunteer army: With a broad coalition established and focused on a compelling vision, it is not difficult to gather the masses. You can employ many techniques. Some that worked for us include engaging your corporate communications department. They are the best at handling caregiver communications. Conspire with them to do even more. You do not want to skimp on expenses here. Create multiple rallies with giveaways. All messaging needs to focus on the change. There should be a way to connect the dots between everyone's job and digital transformation, so it becomes personal. Spend significant time evangelizing the benefits and the reasons why.

Enable action by removing barriers: Another key role of a leader is to remove barriers. Once identified and escalated, you need to act on these immediately. If you take care of small things quickly, it will create an atmosphere of order and keep larger issues from being created. Every obstacle should be quickly reported, considered, and dealt with. This not only helps manage obstacles before they become out of control but also helps build trust that leaders are listening and taking swift action.

Generate short-term wins: We emphasized how digital transformation requires an agile mindset at every phase of the journey. When leveraging agile, quick wins are the norm and will happen as a natural by-product of digital transformation. In non-agile environments, you will need to be proactive. It is critical that the organization notices the velocity of transformation. Again, it builds trust and confidence as well as reinforces the authority to lead. All this is necessary to take out risks associated with culture. The first thing we did was eliminate restrictions on mailbox sizes. This single act alone impacted everyone and eliminated one of the most frustrating aspects associated with IT. With cloud, there was no reason to continue such legacy practices. The goodwill this created bought us another several months to deliver more meaningful aspects of transformation.

Sustain acceleration: With quick wins in place and an abundance of communications, it is time to deliver harder and deeper. This should be a relentless pursuit. While you have success, your detractors are waiting for the momentum to slow and begin harvesting seeds of discord. You worked hard to hear all voices, but some remained silent on purpose. While you may have three to four primary initiatives that were born out of step 3, focus most of your efforts on one of these and deliver beyond expectations. You will need several of these to get over the hump and truly sustain acceleration. Perhaps it will be a digital front door for your patients or ambient voice for clinicians.

Institute change: As evidence of digital transformation mounts, inertia alone will not ensure success. There is more to be done to institutionalize the work and restructure the culture. There is a natural tendency to revert to how we were trained or our own comfort levels. This is something the CEO cannot delegate. The CEO must be very visible and vocal about success to date and how we will revert to the "good ole days." There are no "good ole days." The best days are ahead for all of us serving in healthcare as we adopt digital transformation as a new way of caring.

Key Takeaways and Action Steps

1. Digital transformation has taken on an urgency in the wake of the COVID-19 pandemic that requires healthcare enterprises to make strategic choices quickly and efficiently to serve patient needs in a predominantly virtual mode of care delivery.
2. Having a digital transformation partner can help accelerate change and serve consumers in the new telehealth and virtual care landscape. Invest in robust governance and processes for identifying and managing technology vendors and maximizing the value of technology investments.

4. Chief digital officers need to gain cross-functional buy-in and alignment with IT for success with implementing digital roadmaps and demonstrating sustained value.
5. Consider setting up a digital transformation office that is removed from day to day operational responsibility and can drive enterprise-wide collaboration.
6. Clarity of vision, clear responsibilities, and transparent accountability are requirements for effective governance.
7. Successful digital transformation leaders have an enterprise vision and roadmap, involve stakeholders early, and learn from their peers in the industry.
8. Digital transformation success is predicated on new financial thinking and analysis. Allocating investments in the digital age using old school methods will lead to failure.
9. IT will be challenged to significantly reduce costs while managing increased investment in digital capabilities. This balancing act will determine success or failure.
10. Retreat idea: Convene a meeting of the executive leadership in the organization to address the following questions: What does digital mean to us? What are the enterprise goals with digital transformation? How much should we commit toward digital transformation budgets? How do we track and measure success?

THIRTY-SECOND AGILE CONSULT

Which of Kotter's eight-step process for leading change will be the most challenging to operationalize and why?

Index

AbbVie, 163
ACA, *see* Affordable Care Act
Academic medical centers (AMCs),
129–130, 138
Accelerating digital transformation
in healthcare, 4, 20
Accessible care, 23
Account executive (AE), 185–187
Account management, 185–186
AE, *see* Account executive
Aetna, 29, 32, 43
Affordable Care Act (ACA), 46, 105
Agile digital transformation
blueprint, creating, 63
agile digital transformation
model, 83
digital roadmap development, 77
digital strategy and enterprise
vision, 70–72
prioritization and dependencies,
77–83
readiness assessment and
benchmarking, 72–77
technology platform and partner
selection, 84–92
vision for a digital enterprise,
64–70
Agile methodology, 121–123
AHA, *see* American Hospital
Association

AI, *see* Artificial intelligence
Airline industry, 5
Allscripts, 99, 102, 155, 171
Alphabet, 177
Amazon, 23, 27–28, 155, 172,
176–177
blockchain templates, launch
of, 150
emotion-sensing wearable
device, 145
speech-recognition tool, 144
Amazon Alexa, 43, 145–146
Ambient computing, 131, 143
AMCs, *see* Academic medical
centers
American Hospital Association
(AHA), 8, 104, 174
APIs, *see* Application programming
interfaces
Apple, 3, 23, 27–28, 33, 99, 145,
155, 176
Health app, 52
Application development tools, 36
Application programming interfaces
(APIs), 55, 97, 106–109,
118–119
Argonaut Project, 106
Artificial intelligence (AI), 51, 55,
107, 108, 130–139, 154
Ascension Health, 58, 175, 202

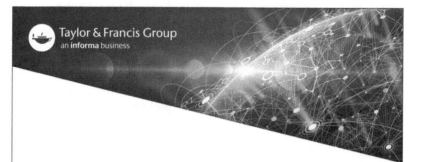

Taylor & Francis eBooks

www.taylorfrancis.com

A single destination for eBooks from Taylor & Francis
with increased functionality and an improved user
experience to meet the needs of our customers.

90,000+ eBooks of award-winning academic content in
Humanities, Social Science, Science, Technology, Engineering,
and Medical written by a global network of editors and authors.

TAYLOR & FRANCIS EBOOKS OFFERS:

A streamlined
experience for
our library
customers

A single point
of discovery
for all of our
eBook content

Improved
search and
discovery of
content at both
book and
chapter level

REQUEST A FREE TRIAL
support@taylorfrancis.com